Blame it on the
DEVON
VICAR

The Curious Conduct of Curates & Clergymen

Tom Hughes

HALSGROVE

ISBN 978 1 84114 861 8

HALSGROVE
Halsgrove House,
Ryelands Industrial Estate,
Bagley Road, Wellington, Somerset TA21 9PZ
Tel: 01823 653777   Fax: 01823 216796
email: sales@halsgrove.com

Part of the Halsgrove group of companies

Information on all Halsgrove titles is available at: www.halsgrove.com
Printed and bound by Shortrun Press, Exeter

Contents

Ten Days a Widower/An Extraordinary Sequel   5
The Rev. Francis Bassett, Rector of Heanton Punchardon

Can't You Forgive Me?   14
The Rev. Anthony Benn, Rector of Woolfardisworthy

The Rectory Governess Scandal   21
The Rev. Henry Raymundo Fortescue, Vicar of East Allington

Caught Off Guard on the Common   32
The Rev. Herbert O. Francis, Curate of Great Torrington

Too Great a Coward   43
The Rev. John Fitzgerald Nagle Gilman, Vicar of Hennock

The Greatest Insult to the Other Sex   55
The Rev. Henry Luxmoore, Vicar of Barnstaple

Scandalously Disgusting & Obscene Letters   65
The Rev. Frederick Luttrell Moysey, Vicar of Sidmouth

The Mysterious Death at the Vicarage   72
The Rev. John Henry Napper Nevill, Vicar of Stoke Gabriel

A Life of Open and Abominable Scandal   81
The Rev. Charles Rookes, Rector of Nymet Rowland

A Flagrant Miscarriage of Justice   92
The Rev. William Ewer Ryan, Vicar of Pilton

An Odious Accusation   101
The Rev. Robert Lane Palmer Samborne, Rector of Ashreigney

Notorious Over All of Exeter   107
Rev. Arthur Whipman, Rector of Gidleigh

His Conduct Has Been Infamous Throughout   116
The Rev. Alfred Baker Winnifrith, Curate of Dalwood

Introduction

A really good clerical scandal, well-spiced and judiciously prolonged …
is worth fifty pounds a week to The Times.
The Churchman's Family Magazine (1863)

No one who examines the great bulk of Victorian clergymen of the Church of England can fail to remark upon their overwhelming piety and propriety; their zeal for their church and their faithful; and their self-less devotion to their calling amidst varying and often quite trying circum-stances. Happily, their stories have been reverently celebrated elsewhere or, perhaps, their overdue recognition shall not come in this temporal world. In this series, however, we recall the clergymen who featured in the numerous clerical scandals of the old Queen's long reign. Let me cede to others the deep and often bitter history of tithe wars, rows over reredos and rubric, churchyard and schoolroom; squabbles that very often became public, personal and quite nasty. Instead, we relate the stories of those cler-gymen whose personal life or family life – whether they be innocent or guilty – would become the subject of scandal and gossip. Adulterers, cads, and cuckolds were found in villages, market towns and even in the cathe-dral close. As one weary Archbishop declared, "You have certain scandals, not arising frequently, but from time to time, and echoed all round the sky until it seems as if the air was full of them." These are the stories from the county of Devon.

ACKNOWLEDGEMENTS

The staff at the British Library, St. Pancras & Colindale: The Lambeth Palace Library and The National Archives, Kew. The editors of Crockford's Clerical Directory. In the USA: The Library of Congress in Washington, DC; the Woodruff Library, Emory University, Atlanta, GA; and the Sterling Memorial Library, Yale University, New Haven CT, USA. I must also thank individually – and most especially, Deborah Gahan, the Local Studies Librarian in Barnstaple. Ms. Gahan was extremely helpful in providing material on the various scandals of North Devon. I owe her great thanks. Additionally, Amanda Bennett, Priaulx, Library, Guernsey; Andrew & Christina Brownsword, owners of the Gidleigh Park Hotel; Brian Carpenter, Archivist, Devon County Council; Maureen Church of the Sidmouth Museum; Amanda Goode, Archivist at Emmanuel College, Oxford; Barbara Griffiths, with help on the Okeden Parry family; Aisling Lockhart, Trinity College, Dublin; Ruth Spires, The Museum of Barnstaple & North Devon. I found the following books quite helpful: *Marital Violence: An English Family History* by Eliza-beth Foyster and *Devon's Amazing Men of God* by Walter Jacobson with an Introduction by Chips Barber. I am extremely grateful for the opportunity and counsel I have received from Simon Butler of Halsgrove Publishing. Finally, I thank my wife, Kathleen McGraw, for all the reasons she knows, and certainly not limited to her excellent proofreading and faultless chauffeuring.

Ten Days a Widower

The Rev. Francis Bassett,
Rector of Heanton Punchardon

&

An Extraordinary Sequel

Involving the 2nd Mrs. Bassett and a Curate

O N A GRAY, windy Thursday, the 12th of January 1877, at the church of St. Augustine in the village of Heanton Punchardon, there was a wedding. If there was more than the usual local interest in these nuptials, it was to be easily explained. For the groom was the rector of the parish, the Rev. Francis William Davie Bassett. As he stood waiting at the altar, around him were memorials and tablets to ancient Bassetts who had long been lords of the manor in Heanton. His bride was Mary Newcombe of Landkey. Adding to the romance of the day, however, was the startling fact that the venerable rector was 74 and Mary but a mere girl of 25, and "hitherto his housekeeper." That final bit of gossip would excite national interest and comment about this quiet ceremony in North Devon. The newspaper headline writers would delight in proclaiming that the Rev. Mr. Bassett had been only TEN DAYS A WIDOWER. The arithmetical reckoning of the journalists was off, but only just. The first Mrs. Bassett had died a fortnight previous, on 28 December 1876.

The Rev. Francis Bassett had been the rector of Heanton Punchardon since taking his degree at Oxford in 1836. Robert de Punchardon had come over with William the Conqueror and eventually settled in North Devon. Some centuries later, the last of the Punchardon males had married a Joan Bassett, and through that son-less marriage, the estates and influence of the Punchardons passed to the Bassetts. The Bassetts had long since occupied Heanton Court and provided many of the rectors at St. Augustine. Both the Court and the church occupy glorious hillside sites overlooking the estuary of the river Taw. The tower of the church, at some ninety feet, is one of the landmarks of the region.

Francis Bassett was born in 1803, the second son of Joseph Davie Bassett, MP, residing at Watermouth Castle, near Ilfracombe. Just before taking up his work at Heanton church, Francis had wed Mary Cartwright of Teignmouth. They had been married nearly fifty years but without any surviving children. In 1876, Mary Bassett fell gravely ill and it was soon plain, there was no hope for her recovery. Mary Newcombe had been a servant in the Bassett home and her role then expanded to be that of a nurse for the rector's dying wife. The old clergyman – himself not in the most robust health - soon grew to rely on the young woman's presence in his household. Regardless, his decision to marry Miss Newcombe, a woman some one-third his age, and in a ceremony conducted not but a few steps from the fresh-turned earth where lay the body of his first wife, could not be viewed as anything less than scandalous. "Astonishment has been caused in Barnstaple," declared the press with some considerable understatement.

Clergymen were not forbidden, certainly, from marrying a member of their household. A Bishop of Norwich had even married his cook (and resigned. So did she.) However, this swift union in Heanton defied the very strict rules of Victorian mourning. Although a widower faced fewer restrictions than a widow, no gentleman could even dare go out into society, let alone remarry within two weeks. Further, was this even a lawful marriage? Under the laws of the Church of England, the banns of marriage had to be read in the church where the man and woman resided on three successive Sundays. Only two Sundays had passed since the demise of the first Mrs. Bassett. However, some older church canons held that the banns had to be read on "three Sundays or holidays (holy days)." Presuming then that the banns were read at St. Augustine's on either, or both, Monday, 1 January, the Feast of the Circumcision, or Saturday, 6 January, the Epiphany, the banns problems arguably could be overcome. Finally, the Rev. Mr. Bassett had some difficulty just finding a clergyman willing to perform the marriage.

The first choice demurred, as he had having presided at the funeral obsequies on the 4th of January. The Rev. Charles Landon, rector of the nearby hamlet of Ashford agreed to marry the couple and rode over to Heanton Punchardon on the 12th of January for that sacred purpose. The aged rector and his young bride appeared publicly for the first time the following Tuesday making a visit to Barnstaple where they were quite the focus of curiosity and comment, much of it likely ribald in nature.

The purpose of the visit to Barnstaple may very well have been to meet with the rector's solicitor, Thomas Hooper Law, at the latter's chambers in Litchdon Street. As mentioned, Mr. Bassett's health was not strong. He suffered from fainting attacks, a malady later traced to epilepsy. He was no longer able to even read the lessons at the church and was turning the great bulk of the parish labours over to a new curate. With that in mind, upon his remarkable marriage, having no children of his own and noting that the other members of his family were all well settled financially (and quite likely put off by this unlikely romance), the rector wished to do something to establish his new wife. He instructed Law to place £4000 in the consols, the "consolidated annuities" funding the national debt, guaranteed by the British government to pay a 3% return per year forever. "Three golden sovereigns on the faith of the British Empire speak for themselves," boasted *The Times*. With the dividends paid twice yearly, the rector and Mary could live comfortably on that interest and upon his death, he planned to leave everything to her.

It was not long after the rector's re-marriage that he surrendered the day-to-day duties at St. Augustine's to his new curate-in-charge, the Rev. David Bernard Davies. Nearly fifty, Welsh-born, educated in Ireland, Davies had most recently been a curate in the adjacent village of Braunton, where he continued to reside with his wife, Mary. The Bassetts and the Davies were often in one another's society and a friendship rapidly developed, "notwithstanding the humble origins" of the second Mrs. Bassett. In addition to his parochial duties, the Rev. Mr. Davies also found the time to engage in secular pursuits, such as the occasional flutter on the London Stock Exchange. He was known to talk of his canny skills as an investor. He liked to disparage the consols and talked of the much greater returns available for those willing to seek them out. While old Rev. Bassett may have been immune to such lure, his young wife proved more susceptible. Mary was asked to come over to the Davies home in Braunton where the curate privately suggested to her that as the old rector continued to fail, she could not be at all sure that the £4000 "in the funds" was to be hers when he passed. The Bassett family would likely "raise a fuss" about such a sum being left to a former servant. It was his opinion, the Rev. Davies advised her, that she should convert the consols into more remunerative investments, especially in the foreign bond issues which had excited a "speculative mania" on the Exchange in the late 1870's. With these newfound profits in her own hands, she would then be secure from the vengeful Bassetts, do what they might.

So it was done. The Rev. Davies scurried off to London to put the sale through. Returning to Heanton, he reported that he had placed £3000 in the Standard Bank and then suggested that "the best thing" would be to use the other £1000 in speculative investments. The details of this arrangement, the curate suggested to Mary, should not be shared with the rector. She assented to this financial counsel and Mr. Davies proceeded to make his investments. In the place of those stodgy consols paying a mere "three gold sovereigns," he purchased Royal Hungarian Gold Rentes paying four percent.

In addition, he threw some money at the Latin American markets, purchasing bonds guaranteed by the governments of Honduras, San Domingo and the Argentine. To be sure, this was not quite the same as being backed by the "faith of the British Empire," but these rapidly expanding new economies were sure to generate exciting profits. It was not likely that Mr. Davies had heard or heeded one MP's warning against "the absurd and false prices which delude a clergyman to invest his money or a widow her savings." That timidity was not for Mr. Davies. He would have instead gladly seconded the un-named broker who told *Fraser's Magazine*, "It is useless to offer £100 consols to a clergyman who wants Honduran bonds at ten per-cent." Lastly, the curate put some of the proceeds from the Bassett's consols in shares of the Great Mysore Indian Gold Mining Company. How could something so grandly titled be anything but a great and rewarding success?

In early 1882, the old rector caught a mortal chill. He lingered through the spring and summer months before breathing his last on 28 September 1882. He was buried at St. Augustine's beside his first wife. At his death, the Rev. Francis Bassett was 79. Mary his widow was now thirty. The Rev. Mr. Davies would have to leave Heanton upon the arrival of the new rector. In 1884, he became the rector of a small parish at Fisherton Delamere in Wiltshire.

When the will of the late Mr. Bassett was read, it went unchallenged. Other than a few small legacies to charities and to longtime servants and church workers, the rest of the estate - including presumably the £4000 in consols, was left to his widow, the second Mary Bassett. Her inheritance having passed to her without any controversy, Mary Bassett began to feel that perhaps it would be better now to find a safer haven for her money. When she went to see Mr. Davies about her investments, he abruptly sent her away. Davies was now claiming that the late Rev. Bassett had authorized the sale of those consols and she had no further claim on that money. In fact, the money was gone; it had been lost in speculative transactions that had proven to be disappointments.

A simple woman, Mary Bassett was left very much at sea. She had lost her home at the rectory and other than what her late husband had left her outside the funds, she was without means of support. Her Bassett in-laws were not at all friendly. There seemed to be no recourse. Falling back upon her skills as a nurse and companion, she moved in with Richard Clogg, a Heanton farmer and the churchwarden during most of the late rector's decades in the village.

Mrs. Clogg was a difficult woman, who suffered from – not to put too fine a point on it – "occasional fits of insanity." Mary Bassett was to tend to her care and needs. Apparently in some conversation with Mr. Clogg, Mary revealed to him the story of her investments and the curt explanation that had been given to her by Mr. Davies. Clogg sent Mary to Messrs Ffinch & Charter, Barnstaple solicitors. On 6 September 1884, the following letter was sent to the Rev. Mr. Davies at his new rectory:

> Mrs. Mary Bassett, widow and executrix of the late Rev. Francis William Davie Bassett, has consulted us with regard to the £4000 in consols which were sold and the proceeds handed to you upon trust for the survivor of her or her husband. She tells us that she has made appeals to you on the subject. We must ask you to say on what day in the course of the week you will be prepared to transfer into her name the sum of £4000 consols and to pay her interest from the date of your selling out the same. In default of your doing this we shall have to consider very seriously the proper steps to take. We are sorry to have to write in this tone, but, according to our instructions, the case is an exceedingly clear one.

The letter went on to contend that Davies had misled Mary about the value of the shares he had purchased, i.e. the Honduran bonds, he valued at £450, were at the time of purchase worth closer to £100. Messrs. Ffinch & Charter expressed the hope that the clergyman had kept all the receipts for the various transactions and would provide them promptly.

The very next day, from Fisherton Delamere rectory, the Rev. Davies replied to the solicitors, in what *The North Devon Journal* called "the following extraordinary manner:"

> In reply to your letter of yesterday's date, I beg to state that I never received any money upon trust from the late Mr. Bassett or from the woman who styles herself his widow and on whose behalf you have written me. You say that from your instructions this case is an exceedingly clear one. Pray let me know what your instructions are and how I owe any anything to this indecent woman. I say indecent because she compelled Mr. Bassett, as he often told me, to go through the ceremony of marriage with her in the week after the decease of his wife, when through overwhelming grief he hardly knew what he was doing; and also because she has been living since the death of Mr. Bassett with a farmer whose wife lives apart from. Living as you do, on the spot, you must be acquainted with these indecencies. I do not owe anything to this woman nor has she ever made any application to me on the subject of her claim. The whole of her story is a tissue of falsehoods. The instrument by which the proceeds of the sale of the consols were handed over to me speaks for itself and shows that value was given and received.
>
> I remain yours faithfully,
> David Bernard Davies

As the solicitors had warned, steps would have to be taken. The case of *Bassett v Davies* was heard in the Chancery Court, London, on 20 March 1885, before Mr. Justice Field. The learned judge called it a "remarkable and disagreeable case" and said he could only hope that the parties could reach an agreement to settle this matter privately. Neither side, however, expressed any willingness to grant the judge's wish and the trial commenced. Mr. John Murphy QC, a corpulent Irishman and popular "man at the bar," said his client, a young widow, had no wish to compromise and no settlement was possible unless the Rev. Mr. Davies made her whole once again. Murphy asserted that it would be for Justice Field to decide which of these two individuals was telling the truth. He suggested that either his client was a complete liar (which, of course, he did not believe) or she had been cruelly victimized by her late husband's stock-jobbing curate. Rev. Davies had cajoled an innocent young woman, a former housemaid, under false pretenses, to turn over to him a sum of not less than £4000. He then lost that money and was now willing to defend himself by telling a story that was "utterly false."

Murphy called outrageous the Rev. Davies's assertion that Mary Bassett was somehow an indecent woman who had conned her way into her employer's life. He led Justice Field through the history of her relationship with the late rector and insisted that the sudden second marriage was an entirely mutual act on their parts. Mr. Bassett had become truly attached to young Mary during his late wife's illness. As an old man, in failing health, he wished her to continue as his caretaker. To avoid scandal and because of his affection for her, their marriage was arranged. Rev. Bassett had proven his affection for his new wife by taking very speedy steps to ensure that she would be financially settled when the day came – and it was not likely to be a distant one – that he would be gone. As for Mary's current residence with the Cloggs, the farmer's wife was unfortunately mad and had to be occasionally placed under confinement. There was no indecency of any kind.

As for the money, Murphy said that the Rev. Mr. Davies had taken advantage of the failing powers of the old rector and the innocence of young Mary Bassett. The curate had invited Mary to come to his home in Braunton. Getting her alone, he filled her mind with talk of speculative riches.

He placed a "power of attorney" before her, which she signed. She was also told to get the signature of her husband, by then, unfortunately, barely lucid. Empowered with this document, the Rev. Davies set at work. Murphy said that all of the transactions had been thoroughly gone into by his investigators. He charged that Mr. Davies had never put any of the proceeds from the sale of the consols into the Standard Bank but had instead used the entire £4000 to open a speculative account at his brokers. For instance, the Honduran bonds were a bust. In *Fenn on the Funds*," a contemporary financial journal, the editor wrote, "It may well be asked how this country [i.e. Honduras] found capitalists in Europe willing to lend it five millions of money." A revolution in San Domingo meant more losses. Murphy said that Davies lost it all, "in a comparatively short period of time." The curate's total losses, including his own stake, were nearer £4500. After her husband's death, Mary went to the Rev. Davies for clarification on the status of her money. He sent her away, telling her she had "feathered her nest enough already." The curate had insisted that the money had been invested at the direction of the Rev. Bassett and she had no claim to it.

On the stand, Mary Bassett displayed a naivete about all matters financial. Toward the end of his life, her husband's mind had been failing and
his "fits" were more numerous. For the most part, he had become incapable
of conducting his business affairs. She had, therefore, placed her entire
trust in the advice she had received from the Rev. Mr. Davies. At his
request, she had gotten her husband to sign the "power of attorney"
authorizing the sale of the consols. After her husband's death, when she
went to the curate he rebuked her and sent her away. She couldn't go to her
husband's solicitor because he had also died. She felt that she had been
taken advantage of. John Forbes, the counsel for Rev. Davies, coaxed from
Mary the admission that she had no copy of this "power of attorney." She
also conceded that through the investments managed by the Rev. Davies
she had received some small returns from her mining stocks. Good news,
perhaps, from the Mysore digs in the distant Raj?

The state of the Rev. Mr. Bassett's mind at the time of the consols sale
was key to the case. Dr. Stephen Orson Lane, the Braunston physician who
had treated Rev. Bassett, was called to provide his expert analysis. In his
opinion, the clergyman could not have been too greatly involved in such
complicated matters.

Nonetheless, in defense of the Rev. Davies, attorney Forbes argued that
the transaction involving the consols had been solely between the old rector
and his curate. The Rev. Bassett, anxious to have money put aside for his
new wife, had purchased the consols. However, he had held some conversations with his curate, knowing as he did that Mr. Davies had enjoyed
some success on the exchange. The rector was "desirous of making similar
investments." There was no "power of attorney" ever signed; it was simply
on the verbal authorization of the Rev. Bassett that the consols were to be
sold and re-invested. And, as almost an afterthought, Davies agreed to also
handle Mrs. Bassett's £200 in the Indian mines, for which she had been
earning her return. As for the Rev. Bassett's £4000, sadly, the speculative
investments had come a-cropper. The brokerage house employed by Mr.
Davies (Messrs Stokes & Hall of Telegraph St. EC London) had been forced
into liquidation. The money was gone. It was most unfortunate but those
losses came out of the Bassett estate and, upon the rector's death, the
monies that he had hoped to pass on to his young widow were gone. Mrs.
Bassett had no claim against Mr. Davies. It was the way of the exchange:
investments, unfortunately, cannot be guaranteed to bring a profit and, in
fact, may be lost entirely.

The morning session had ended with Dr. Lane's testimony. The physician's opinion on the decline of Rev. Bassett's mental powers had been

hurtful to the curate's case. After a luncheon break, Mr. Forbes returned to court to tell Justice Field that the Rev. Davies "appreciates the gravity of the issues raised" against him. They were now ready to offer a settlement to Mary Bassett. However, as part of that offer, she would have to return to the Rev. Davies the profitable mining stocks that he had purchased for her. He could not be held responsible only for all the losses; if there were gains, they must redound to him. Mr. Murphy rejected the offer. If the defense wishes to give up, let them say so plainly. Mrs. Bassett was unwilling to accept a farthing less than £3945 plus interest and all court costs.

Justice Field said the case had troubled him greatly; there were two very different versions of events before him. It was for him to decide which was the more believable. A rustic clergyman, of declining mental capacities, and his wife - "hitherto a servant" - had been led to make speculative investments by the defendant, a clergymen in whom they had some reason to trust. The investments had been made in dubious ventures. The result was that the great bulk of the money was gone. That was a fact. There was no documentary evidence; no "power of attorney" was ever produced. In the end, Field said he was compelled to rule that Mrs. Bassett should win her action against the erstwhile curate of Heanton. Rev. Davies was ordered to make full restoration of the monies lost.

Of course, as will quite often occur in such matters, a court judgment is not the same as seeing the money appear in the bank. The Rev. Mr. Davies was soon in bankruptcy. He lost his church in Fisherton Delamere; the living there had been purchased for him by his wife but she died suddenly and he was forced to withdraw. No more church openings came his way. As late as 1896, the stock-jobbing curate was still in bankruptcy court, pleading his numerous losses owing to "rash and hazardous speculations."

Poor Mary Bassett; she likely never saw any of that money again. Since it was intended to be the bulk of the legacy from her late husband, she was left with pretty much nothing. It is a reasonable surmise – but not a certainty – that she was the Mary from Landkey who was later married (or living with) a local farmer named Conibear. The marriage was not registered. They had three children.

Can't You Forgive Me?

The Rev. Anthony Benn
Rector of Woolfardisworthy

THERE ARE many villages of the same name scattered across England. Uptons, Suttons, and Nortons, for instance, dot the landscape. There are, however, only two villages with the unusual old English name of Woolfardisworthy. To have located these two villages in the same county seems to be needlessly perverse, yet so it is in Devon. Adding to the confusion, the name of both villages is pronounced, and sometimes spelt, "Woolsery." There is a Woolfardisworthy in North Devon, near Bideford. There is a Woolfardisworthy in South Devon, six miles northwest of Crediton. It is in this latter village that the Rev. Anthony Benn came to be rector in 1866.

This Woolfardisworthy is quite the smaller of the two communities with no more than two hundred residents. Tiny St. Mary's church had been completely restored in the 1840's by a nephew of the great Charles Barry, designer of the new Palace of Westminster. The rectory was also new, built in a Tudor Gothic style to match the church. It was known as the "Old Rectory" when visited by the intrepid Mr. Pevsner in the 20th Century and he took time to note the "nice iron gatespiers and gate."

The Rev. Mr. Benn was the son of a naval officer, Capt. Thomas Benn, who – thanks to the long peace - had not been to sea since 1815. Anthony had been educated at Cheltenham School and then at Emmanuel College, Cambridge, where he rowed for the Cantabs in the 1857 boat race. Alas, the

Oxford boat had much the better of it, finishing a good 30 seconds before young Benn and his mates. After his ordination, he spent the requisite years as a curate before being appointed to the rectory at Woolfardisworthy in 1866.

He took up his duties in the company of his new wife. Rev. Benn was thirty on his wedding day; Mary Elizabeth Mansel was just seventeen. She was an excellent catch for the clergyman. Mary was the oldest of six children, all of them born in India, to Charles Grenville Mansel, who had "earned a high reputation as one of the ablest financiers in India." From his beginnings as a local magistrate and tax collector, he had risen to be a top financial strategist to the Raj, serving in Calcutta and lastly with Sir Henry Lawrence in the Punjab. In 1855, before the Mutiny, Mansel retired, and came home to England to live as a true wealthy "nabob." His daughter and the new rector of Woolfardisworthy were married in London in September 1866.

Charles, the first of their two sons was born the following July. It was a difficult confinement and Mary was left quite weak. She also grew quickly to be discontented with her lot in the quiet village. In January 1869, the rector's father passed away at his home in Upper Norwood, near Croydon. Rev. Benn, the heir, would be much involved in settling the old captain's affairs. Rather than leaving Mary behind in the "dull" village, she and their son accompanied him to Croydon, where Anthony's eldest sister had kept house for her father. Once in London, however, Mary was no happier; she was pregnant again and had decided that the seaside was the place for her to build the strength needed to avoid the trauma of her first delivery. She pleaded with Anthony to be allowed to go to Brighton, in the company of friends. He agreed to this.

Mary remained in Brighton for most of a year. Her husband, who frankly does not seem to have been the most attentive of spouses, arrived in that seaside town in early 1870 hoping to reclaim his wife (and their second son, Herbert) and return with her to Devon. Mary begged his indulgence again, insisting that the climate had been restorative and she would so very much wish to remain in the bracing air (and bracing society) of Brighton a little longer. Her friends had long since returned to London, but her family was nearby and her brother stood guard as her escort and protector. The Rev. Mr. Benn agreed to this arrangement and took a suite for his wife and young Mansel at the then famous Lion Mansion Hotel, facing the sea on the Grand Junction Parade. He then bid his wife farewell and returned to Woolfardisworthy, where after his absence following the death of his father, parish affairs had conspired to make him very busy indeed.

Nevertheless, he was pained at this continuing separation. The Rev. Benn had an idea: wouldn't his wife equally enjoy the seaside in Devon's own Torquay, to be sure much more convenient to his parsonage than Sussex. Mary agreed to consider such a move and was to meet Anthony in Torquay in April of 1870. At the last moment, however, she claimed to be too weak to make the long journey.

The disappointment was too much for the long-suffering husband and cleric to stand. He was finally bestirred to put his boot down. He went off to Brighton and pleaded with Mary to come home with him. She refused, insisting that the village and the rectory were too dull for her tastes. Coincidentally, Mr. Benn had the gathering sense that Brighton was altogether too exciting for his. He was especially concerned with the number of young officers from the Hussars billeted in the city for the season. Apparently, one or two favourites of Mrs. Benn had been known to dine with her. The Rev. Benn was by now convinced that young Mansel was entirely unsuitable as an escort. The rector did at last decree that Mary could only remain in Brighton if her mother came to stay with her.

In addition, Mary would have to leave the officer-rich environment of Lion's Mansion for cheaper lodgings at King's boarding house. Ensuring that his edict was to be obeyed, Mr. Benn returned to Woolfardisworthy and Mary's Brighton interlude dragged merrily on.

Her mother having been called home to Guernsey, Mary was forced to quit Brighton at last. She returned to her husband at the rectory in Woolfardisworthy. There she remained amid the torpid rhythms of the summer ecclesiastical calendar. Happily, she was offered an escape. Her dear friends, the Knightons, had taken a place at Southend-on-Sea and begged the Rev. Mr. Benn to allow Mary a chance to come all the way to the Essex coast for a break. The compliant clergyman authorized such a move. She traveled, via London, and remained with the Knightons for some little time, or did she? When Mary returned to Woolfardisworthy, Mr. Benn was curious to know why her luggage tags indicated that she had been to Bognor. Mary assured him that it was undoubtedly the fault of a careless railway porter. This seemed to mollify the rector.

It must be said that Mr. Benn seemed too easily distracted from his duties in Woolfardisworthy. Soon, he and Mary were off to stay at Ryde on the Isle of Wight, again to the seaside for the benefit of her health. Nor did he long remain on the island. He had to (occasionally at least) put in an appearance in the parish before catching a train to Scotland for some shooting. Mary, meanwhile, went to Guernsey to be with her family. She was to join him in Scotland for a wedding in Berwick that fall.

This charade of a marriage, during which they had been together perhaps less than half the time, was beginning to unravel. The Rev. Mr. Benn had now heard disquieting reports of his wife's dalliance with a particular officer in the Hussars while in Brighton that spring and summer. In Berwick, there was a dispute and Mary left peremptorily. The holidays were spent apart and in February 1871, the Rev. Benn summoned his wife to meet him in Brighton. She arrived, in the company of her father, with whom Mr. Benn continued to have a strong relationship. The rector had taken the time to draw up a formal list of questions for his wife that he presented to her. Of course, she was not required to answer; however, her silence would have alarming implications for their marriage. Mary agreed to answer the questions.

Mary Benn insisted to her husband that she had not been unfaithful with the officer in question. Anthony knew the man; in Brighton, he had been part of a dinner party that the officer had also attended. Mary confessed, however, that she had dined with the officer on several other occasions. She admitted that he had been to her suite to dine alone. Mary told her husband that she had taken no gifts from the officer but she had purchased the Captain, for he held that somewhat exalted rank, a set of shirt studs. The Rev. Benn said he was well aware of all the dinners and the studs, since those bills had come to his account for payment. These were among the incidents that triggered his suspicions. She had the dates wrong for her stay with the Knightons in Southend. She insisted the letters she had received there had come from her brother. Anthony bluntly asked if she could persist in denying that she had been intimate with that man? At that point, Mary begged her father to leave the room. Alone with her husband, she burst into tears. She admitted that she had been with the Captain in Brighton, Worthing, London and, of course, Bognor. But it was now over. She pleaded, "Christ forgave the woman taken in adultery. Can't you forgive me?" Her answer came quickly. The Rev. Anthony Benn left Brighton directly to return to Woolfardisworthy.

As Mr. Benn had been slow to suspect his wife's infidelity, he was even more dilatory in dealing with it. They had separated, of course. Mr. Benn had also resigned from St. Mary's, Woolfardisworthy. An auction was announced "of the property of the Rev. A. Benn who is about to leave the rectory." Having disposed of "two large slip pigs nearly fit for the butcher" and "farm implements nothing worse for use," he could then turn his attention to ridding himself of a wife. The formal request for a divorce was not heard until 20 November 1873, more than two years having passed since Mary's tearful confession.

Frederick Inderwick was beginning a career that would see him rise to the pinnacle of the divorce bar; in the future, he would most often stand with the betrayed wife. In this case, he spoke for the Rev. Anthony Benn. The parties involved were all quite wealthy and could afford the finest counsel. Dr. Thomas Spinks QC represented Mrs. Benn. The legendary Serjeant-at-Law William Ballentine held a brief for Capt. Uvedale Okeden Parry Okeden-Parry, of the 18th Hussars and Turnworth Hall, Dorset. The delay taken by Mr. Benn in bringing the action had also allowed the Captain the time to get married; in 1871, he wed the daughter of a prominent clergyman (!), the Rev. Henry Lee-Warner of Walsingham Abbey, Norfolk. The Captain was at present serving with his regiment in India and he had declined to return for the proceedings. A mysterious second co-respondent had been added to the case against Mrs. Benn, a gentleman known only as "Mr. Whiston" who had allegedly committed adultery with her in Worthing.

Addressing Sir James Hannen, the President of the Divorce Court, and a jury of Londoners, Inderwick said that the Rev. Benn was a clerical gentleman of considerable property. He had married Mary Elizabeth Mansel, eldest daughter of a gentleman possessing an Indian fortune. Married in 1866, the couple had two sons. Mrs. Benn had expressed her displeasure with life in Woolfardisworthy. Her confinements had been strenuous and her husband graciously allowed her to seek her strength in Brighton and other watering places, having financed all of that, of course. In Brighton, she made the acquaintance of Capt. Okeden-Parry. Mary was, of course, born in India. Capt. Okeden-Parry's father had been in the Bengal Civil Service. There was that, then, in common. The officers of the various Hussar regiments that passed through Brighton were in great demand socially, and it was quite natural that this friendship might have been formed. The Rev. Benn had even dined with Capt. Okeden-Parry on one occasion. However, disquieting reports as to his wife's conduct had begun to reach Mr. Benn at Woolfardisworthy. These reports had, sadly, been proven true. Mr. Benn had heard the truth from his wife's own lips. She had confessed to him. She had been unfaithful to her husband at the Lion's Mansion in Brighton, at a hotel in Bognor, and in London. In the latter case, she admitted meeting Capt. Okeden-Parry in London for the theatre. After the play ended, he said that he had missed his last train. She agreed to allow him to stay with her at the Great Western Hotel at Paddington. He took an adjoining room. Inderwick reminded Sir James Hannen what the great judge Sir William Scott had said. "Confession stands high, or should I say, highest, in the scale of evidence." But it was not enough. It would be Mr. Inderwick's duty to present the witnesses to Mrs. Benn's adultery.

Charlotte Tomlinson, Mrs. Benn's lady's maid, testified that Capt. Okeden Parry had called frequently at their suite, often staying until nearly midnight. She identified a photograph of the absent officer. Her mistress and the captain "dined" privately and strict instructions were left that they must not be interrupted. On one occasion, Charlotte was given a rare evening off and when she returned she learned that the Captain had been there for most of the evening. The servant recalled being frequently given letters to be delivered to the Captain. The officer's counsel, Mr. Ballentine won from Miss Tomlinson the admission that Capt. Okeden-Parry was not the only officer to pay calls upon Mrs. Benn. Many did. Mrs. Benn and her brother had entertained frequently. Nor was the Captain always alone in his visits. Ballentine also reminded the court that Miss Tomlinson remained in the employ of the Rev. Mr. Benn.

Henry Dyer, one of the waiters at the Lion Mansion Hotel, said he had walked in unexpectedly on the two parties and found them on a couch in a position that no married woman should find herself with another gentleman.

Mrs. Knighton had also come to court; she was the friend who had invited Mary Benn to Southend-on-Sea in the summer of 1870. Mary had cut short her stay suddenly and said she had been called home to Wool-fardisworthy. Those dates coincided with the balls-up over the baggage at Bognor. Sarah Browning was a chambermaid at the Norfolk Hotel on the Esplanade in Bognor. She recognized Mrs. Benn and, from the photograph, Capt. Okeden-Parry as the people who had taken adjoining suites, rooms 14 and 15, on the weekend in question.

That closed the case for the Rev. Mr. Benn. The lawyer for Mrs. Benn chose not to defend the action. She had, after all, admitted it. Ballentine, however, said the gallant, if absent, Captain admitted nothing. It was mistaken identity of the part of the witnesses who had been heard from. The witnesses – although they said they recognized the Captain's photo-graph – had been unable to correctly state his height, the colour of his hair, etc. Capt. Okeden-Parry certainly did not deny knowing Mrs. Benn. Both had roots in India, the Captain's regiment was currently there. Their friendship was a social one. Ballentine suggested that a parade of young officers had been entertained in her suite at the Lion Mansion Hotel. What kind of a husband leaves his young wife alone in Brighton, of all places, crawling with officers and dandies? This pretty, wealthy woman of 20 was alone at a hotel and a boarding house with no more protection than her 18-

year old brother? Ballentine managed to severely rattle the poor chambermaid from Bognor into admitting she couldn't really describe the Captain's clothes or features. Ballentine said there was not a shred of proof that his client was even in Bognor at the time in question.

Inderwick reminded his honourable friend that if Capt. Okeden-Parry wished to contest this case, he could have made himself available for this court. Since the officer chose not to leave his regiment, the identity questions were his to rue from afar.

Still, there was always the mysterious "Mr. Whiston." Was he the fall guy? Did the Rev. Mr. Benn agree to allow Capt. Okeden-Parry to walk away unstained, and, instead, throw the charge that his wife had also committed adultery with a second man? Both Inderwick and Ballentine insisted to Justice Hannen that no deals had been made.

Summing up for the jury, Hannen said that the evidence was beyond doubt that Mrs. Benn had committed adultery, but with whom? Reasonable doubt had been raised to bring into question the claim that her lover had been Capt. Uvedale Okeden-Parry. The jury must decide. In fact, the jury did find that Mary Benn had committed adultery with Capt. Okeden-Parry and *vice versa*. The jury also wished to state they did not believe that the Rev. Benn had been guilty of cruelty towards his wife. While not raised at any length, Mr. Ballentine thought that the rector's indifference to his wife's whereabouts and his willingness to live for long periods of time without her (and her consortium) were grounds for a counter-claim of cruelty. Regardless, her husband's disinterest had very likely contributed to her unhappiness and her fall.

Mary Benn remarried soon after her divorce. Her new husband was Thomas de Saumurez, a Guernsey solicitor and member of one of that island's leading families. They had a large family.

As for her supposed lover, Capt. Uvedale Okeden Parry Okeden-Parry, his marriage to Miss Lee-Warner survived the scandal but his young wife died in childbirth soon after the trial. He then married Caroline Hambro, daughter of a wealthy merchant banker.

The Rev. Mr. Anthony Benn never re-married. It does seem that his heart was never really in his first marriage. His divorce finalized, he settled in Herefordshire, purchasing Pudleston Court, "a handsome modern mansion in the castellated style." He lived there with his two sons. Benn remained a "clergyman without cure of souls" until his death in 1904. Charles, his elder son inherited the estate; Herbert – the younger – emigrated to New Zealand where he died in 1911. There is a memorial to Herbert in Woolfardisworthy church.

The Rectory Governess Scandal

The Rev. Henry Raymundo Fortescue, Vicar of East Allington

THE FORTESCUES have for centuries been among the great families of Devon. During the anti-Royalist wars of the 17th Century, Sir Edmund held the castle at Salcombe for his King. When the fortress finally fell in 1645, he was allowed – by way of tribute – to leave and take the castle key along with him. Sir Edmund then marched the nine miles north to Fallapit, the family seat at the village of East Allington.

The village lies in the beautiful South Hams, that section of Devon between the sea and Dartmoor. The climate is among the mildest in England, protected from the north winds by the higher ground at Dartmoor. Fortescue fortunes have thrived in East Allington and, in the words of the great Devonian antiquarian, the Rev. Sabine Baring-Gould, "their monuments crowd the parish church." Two centuries after doughty Sir Edmund's return, a Fortescue was still in residence at Fallapit; the house having since been rebuilt "in the midst of extensive and tasteful pleasure grounds." William Blundell Fortescue was the lord of the manor. Meanwhile, William's brother, the curiously named Rev. Henry Raymundo Fortescue was the rector of that parish church of St. Andrew.

The hillside church is not surprisingly also dominated by the Fortescues. The early twentieth century ecclesiologist – vernacularly known today as a "church crawler" - John Stabb catalogued the family memorials, shields and marveled at "the rood screen [which] is finely carved in very dark oak and bears the arms of the Fortescues." Our story begins, then, on a Sunday in June of 1852. Standing in front of the family coat of arms, the Rev. Mr. Fortescue publicly turned a parishioner away from the communion rail. This sacramental rebuke could not fail to cause a scene in such a small village: all the more so, of course, because the victim was no less a personage than Capt. E.H. Delafosse, a retired naval officer and, by the way, also one of the churchwardens at St. Andrew's.

More than a few of the worshippers in attendance on that Sabbath day were already well aware of what was afoot in East Allington. It had understandably been the topic of much discussion at the local pub, *The Fortescue Arms* (what else?) Reports of the Captain's amorous exploits with the local maidens were an oft-told tale in the village. Word of one such report had reached the ears of the rector's wife. Hearing the gossip and rumour about the failings of one parishioner or another was perhaps an occupational hazard of a country clergyman's wife. In one of his *Addresses Delivered on Various Occasions*, the Rev. Francis Pigou had warned of the dangers of dabbling in such idle talk:

> Shall I speak of the vice of tittle-tattle and gossip, of the irreparable mischief that may be done in a parish by a busy and careless tongue? ... It is fatal to confidence, and to all that good understanding which should subsist between a pastor and his people, if his wife make her visits the occasion for tittle-tattle and gossip about her neighbours; if, instead of putting on the best construction, she puts on the worst ...
>
> By her above all should this be realised:
>
> *Believe not each accusing tongue,*
> *As some weak people do.*
> *But ever hope that story false.*
> *Which ought not to be true.*

Well put, indeed, by the Rev. Pigou, the Rural Dean of Halifax. That said, however, Mrs. Fortescue would certainly have received even Mr. Pigou's blessing for reporting this bit of gossip back to her husband. It was one thing for Capt. Delafosse to play the lothario with a farm girl. While censurable on the officer's part, the Rev. Fortescue might excuse his church-warden that level of misconduct. However, the clergyman could hardly administer the sacrament to the man he had earlier that week accused of "criminal intercourse" with the rectory governess.

A bit of potted biographical information about the captain. Edward Hollingworth Delafosse was a man of 64. London-born, he had gone to sea as a youth. As a midshipman, he had served in Nelson's fleet at Copenhagen. Later, as a lieutenant, he'd been mentioned in the dispatches for "several gallant exploits" in the Adriatic, during one of which he was wounded. He later commanded a frigate at the Battle of Algiers. Then, during the long Victorian peace, he took his half-pay and settled into a comfortable country retirement at Rimpstone, his home in East Allington. The captain and his wife, Sophia, had no children.

As a churchwarden and an adornment to local society, the captain, and his wife, of course, moved in the highest circles in East Allington. Such as they were. The directory for 1850 lists only the vicar, his brother at Fallapit House, Capt. Delafosse and one other "gentleman," a Mr. Luscombe. There were as many blacksmiths as gentlemen in the small rural community. The Delafosses would have often enjoyed the hospitality of the growing Fortescue family at the handsome rectory. The 33-year old rector and his wife Ellen had five children, three sons and two daughters. Percival, the oldest, was nine. The children were under the daily care and instruction of their governess, 27-year old Miss Mary Ann Pitt. In the spring of 1852, at a time when the clergyman was away on business, Mrs. Fortescue was apprised of some village gossip linking her governess with the dashing, if much older, naval officer. Summoning Miss Pitt into her study, Mrs. Fortescue asked if these reports she had received were accurate. The governess broke down completely and confessed. The rector's wife said that Miss Pitt would have to leave the rectory immediately. On the 7th of June 1852, the young woman was packed off to her sister, a Mrs. Fanny Willes, who also received as many as three letters from Mrs. Fortescue explaining the disgraceful conduct that had resulted in Miss Pitt's summary dismissal from the rectory at East Allington.

Such conduct, even if only suspected or gossiped about, could not be countenanced in any person holding such a vital household position as a governess - let alone in a clergyman's establishment. Madame Bureaud-Riofrey, the wife of a French born doctor but "an English lady of high mental attainments," turned out a series of books on the proper way for parents to select and observe a governess. In 1843, she wrote, in a book entitled, *Moral & Intellectual Education*:

It is not to be expected that these parents should give up all of their control; but if they really love their children they take more than usual care to place right-minded persons with them; I know that objections may be made to what I now state, but I also know that in order to make good Christians, children must be early accustomed to the practice of virtue, for virtuous principles are intimately connected with early affections ... I expressly repeat that example is most powerful in early age, when the mind and manners are unformed; consequently the most certain method of ensuring a right education is to place young children under the direction of *a governess who in all respects may serve as a model.*

Miss Mary Ann Pitt had apparently proven to be no such model for the young Fortescues.

Upon the rector's return to East Allington, he was, of course, to be fully briefed on this domestic unpleasantness by his good wife. Mr. Fortescue felt it to be incumbent upon him to then confront his friend and church-warden with these facts and demand an explanation for his conduct. Captain Delafosse indignantly denied that he had mis-conducted himself in the slightest way with Miss Pitt. He demanded that the governess be brought to him to explain her supposed confession. When told that she had already been sent away, Delafosse declared, "Well, then, she leaves your house as pure as she came into it, as far as I'm concerned." He also expressed his dismay that the clergyman would listen to the gossip of a few village yokels and accept it over the word of an officer of Her Majesty's navy. The Rev. Fortescue withstood these verbal broadsides and informed the Captain that he could no longer be a communicant at St Andrew's and must worship elsewhere. Hence, as already detailed, when Mr. Delafosse presented himself the next Sabbath day at the altar rail at the parish church, he was publicly cut by the rector.

Such an insult, seen by, well, dozens of people, demanded satisfaction. In March 1853, in a case called before Justice William Erle at the Western assizes in Exeter, Captain Delafosse sued the Rev. Fortescue and the rector's wife for slander and libel; the latter charge involving the letters sent to Mrs. Willes. The captain was represented by Charles Butt QC and a young Devon lawyer named John Duke Coleridge, the future Lord Chief Justice. Mr. Butt said every effort had been made to avoid the necessity of a public airing of this matter but as the Fortescues had chosen to listen to the "foolish gossip" of a few villagers rather than the word of an officer and their longtime friend, the matter had sadly arrived now before this court. Capt. Delafosse asked for no money, merely the restoration of his honoured name.

Mr. Butt called, at first, Fanny Willes to establish her receipt of the letters. The letters were lengthy and, in some detail, described the circumstances of the reported "criminal intercourse" between the Captain and her sister, Miss Pitt. These letters were then read to the jury. Mrs. Willes admitted under cross-examination that, after receiving the letters from Mrs. Fortescue, she had gone directly to East Allington. Whilst there, she spoke with the rector's wife, the rectory cook and others and was convinced that the charge contained in the letters was true. "I then felt no doubt of my sister's guilt."

The attorney for Capt. Delafosse told the court he would not call any more witnesses for the moment. Mr. Richard Crowder QC, representing the Fortescues, opened by assuring the court that, for the sake of public decency, the defendants also had no wish to go into the unsavory details of this matter. By bringing this action, the Captain had served to give further publicity to the disgrace meted out to a young woman who might have otherwise been allowed to quietly depart East Allington. Crowder also noted that his friend Mr. Butt had chosen not to call Capt. Delafosse or Miss Pitt to testify until they had heard the defense case first. Crowder suggested that was hardly the strategy that would be employed by any counsel confident in his client's innocence. It would then be his reluctant duty, Crowder declared, to present several witnesses who would make absolutely clear that the statements made by the Rev. and Mrs. Fortescue to and about Capt. Delafosse were true and that the rector and his wife were justified in taking the actions they had. A literal parade of East Allington villagers served as witnesses for their vicar. It seemed as if everyone in East Allington had there eye on the Captain and Miss Pitt.

One local man said he had seen them together some forty times. The schoolmistress, who had employed Miss Pitt as a writing instructor, said that Mary Ann often left her duties unfinished to walk with the Captain. More witnesses with similar evidence followed. However, the witnesses of the greatest interest were three individuals who alleged to have seen the supposed lovers in compromising places and situations.

The first was the village storekeeper, John Pitwood, who testified that he had seen the Captain and Miss Pitt together in one of the numerous old quarries that dot the landscape near East Allington. Pitwood did not deny that he had been spying on them; "in consequence of the rumours" he'd heard. He'd taken it upon himself to follow (stalk?) the couple, knowing the Captain's reputation. He had seen them both furtively arrive at a quarry, finding a low area several feet below ground. He swore they remained there as long as two hours and he crept close enough to see them lying together. When the couple finally emerged from their hideaway, they quickly separated. The captain saw Pitwood that day and attempted to explain that they had been looking for some of the Fortescue children, whom he called "young rogues."

A young fellow named William Pinhay, a farmer's son, was next in the witness box to tell the court that he had seen Mr. Delafosse and the governess in a field near Kellerton Cross. It was the 4th of May, the previous springtime. She was lying down and the captain was near her on his knees. Pinhay had watched the two of them as they carefully checked to ensure that the coast was clear. Pinhay, like Pitwood, was nonetheless able to sneak up on them. But, as he crept closer, Pinhay said he couldn't help but start laughing. He testified that Capt. Delafosse immediately leapt to his feet and was forced to readjust his trousers. Miss Pitt appeared much embarrassed to be seen in such a compromising situation.

Finally, the rectory cook, Harriett Ireland, was sworn to tell of the captain's frequent visits to the Fortescue's home. While, as already stated, such social calls are understandable in village society, Harriet thought that his visits had increased with the arrival of Miss Pitt. The captain had contrived to spend more and more time in the schoolroom with the governess and the children. On one day, when the Fortescues and Mrs. Delafosse had gone over to Totnes, Harriet saw Mary Ann and the captain in the rectory grounds behind a hedge. She managed to get close enough to see, that although both of them were standing up at the time, a "criminal intercourse" was taking place. Whether truly or falsely depicted as lovers, the Captain and the governess were certainly very careless in protecting their privacy.

Harriet, the cook, testified that she had spoken with Miss Pitt about her conduct and the governess, at first, denied it. But after the shopkeeper Pitwood's revelations, Mary Ann became quite upset and said to the cook, "What shall I do, take a cup of poison?" Harriet said Mrs. Fortescue came to her, at last, and said, "Cook, I must know the truth." Harriet testified that she told her mistress that the stories were all true, because "I saw it myself." Harriet was put through a tough series of questions by counsel for Capt. Delafosse. She denied she was a village busybody who told tales on everyone. Harriet indignantly denied that she had ever told anyone that "Master Percvial was born seven months after his mother's (Mrs. Fortescue) marriage!"

The Rev. Mr. Fortescue followed his cook into the witness box. He had always placed the greatest confidence in Miss Pitt as a governess. However, upon his return to East Allington, he had learned from his wife all about this new and most troubling scandal within his own rectory. He had completely supported his wife's action in dismissing the governess immediately. He went next to see Capt. Delafosse. Mr. Fortescue recalled that the captain strongly insisted that "nothing criminal" had taken place. The rector thought such a statement was unsatisfactory. They shook hands and parted. The rector then went to Pitwood and the cook to hear their stories. He then went back to the captain to say that he believed these stories about his conduct with Miss Pitt to be true and their relationship, including his church duties, were at an end. Delafosse demanded to see Miss Pitt immediately. Rev. Fortescue instead suggested that the captain might better confront Pitwood and Pinhay, eyewitnesses to his adultery. The captain had replied that his word as an officer and a gentleman should carry more weight than the tattletale stories of a shopkeeper and a farmhand.

The rector's wife, Ellen Fortescue, took the stand next. She said she had first learned of the reports that her governess had become involved with Delafosse through a conversation with Mr. Pitwood. The storekeeper had also put her in touch with young Pinhay. In her husband's absence, she felt she had to act independently and quickly for the sake of her children. She confronted Miss Pitt: "How came you to meet him in the pit?" The rector's wife testified that the governess almost immediately confessed to everything, sobbing that her "character" had been lost for certain. Mrs. Fortescue recalled that when she told Miss Pitt that she would have to leave the rectory immediately, the governess pleaded for some brief grace period lest everyone know that she had been sent packing in sin and disgrace. Mrs. Fortescue would not hear of it and directly sent the young woman home to her sister. When Capt. Delafosse came to the rectory to protest, she asked him to leave immediately. Mrs. Fortescue freely admitted writing the alleged "libelous" letters to Mrs. Willes. The woman had then come to East Allington and stayed at the rectory for two nights. Mrs. Willes had also gone to Rimpstone to see the captain. When she returned, Mrs. Fortescue recalled that the woman told her that Mr. Delafosse had said to her, in a very confidential way, "Depend upon it, I shall do something for her," meaning, of course, Miss Pitt.

The defendants having made their case, Mr. Butt, the counsel for Capt. Delafosse, as expected, declared his intention to call the two principles to testify. The first to be examined was Miss Mary Ann Pitt. She admitted to having frequently been in the captain's company as he was often at the rectory socially or on church business. As he was very fond of the Fortescue children, and they enjoyed his company as much, Capt. Delafosse would ordinarily visit the schoolroom. While she may have met him while out walking, it was always by happenstance and never by assignation. With five children, two of them toddlers, some assistance in keeping an eye on them all would never be unappreciated. In fact, what the cook saw was Capt. Delafosse helping to lift her over the rectory hedge to round up the youngest of the family. As for the quarry, it was hard to walk anywhere around East Allington without coming near one.

She swore, that on the occasion that Pitwood had told about, she had been walking towards Rimpstone to tell the Captain that the children could not come out that day as planned. She met him on the way. As it was a long walk and she had a bad leg, he asked her to sit for a while and remained with her for no longer than a quarter of an hour. Nothing improper happened on that day or any other time between them. On the occasion described by Pinhay, it was a wet and windy day and she had met the Captain near Kellerton Cross. He had dismounted to speak with her. She was not lying down. He was not lying down. He was certainly not on his knees. He had never even so much as kissed her. Certainly, she and Capt. Delafosse had never had "criminal intercourse." She had never admitted any such improprieties to Mrs. Fortescue. When confronted by the rector's wife, she had angrily denied any wrongdoing. As for the remarks about losing her "character," she knew immediately that to be suddenly turned out of the rectory on such false charges could only ruin her reputation.

Cross examined by Crowder, Miss Pitt admitted that she and the captain very probably had been seen together out walking on more than one occasion. Many times, the Fortescue bairns were with her. On the occasions when she might have been alone, she and the captain met in the casual way so common to life in a small village. Crowder then raised the matter of a Lt. Ross who had visited East Allington and spent the night at the rectory, when both Mr. and Mrs. Fortescue were away. Miss Pitt admitted that she had allowed the young man to stay at the rectory. The full complement of rectory servants had been present that day and through that night and no one could accuse of her any impropriety with Ross. Miss Pitt insisted that she and the lieutenant had merely shared tea and he left the next day. Despite her innocent depiction of Ross' visit, Miss Pitt conceded that she had never mentioned it to her employers.

Capt. Edward Hollingworth Delafosse was next; he swore on his oath as an officer and a gentleman that he had never taken any liberties with

Miss Pitt. There was an innocent explanation for everything. He related the same story as Miss Pitt about the rest stop in the quarry that Pitwood had observed. What the cook saw was the Captain lifting Miss Pitt through a gap in the rectory hedge so she could round up the ever wandering Fortescue brood. The day described by young Pinhay was one that he had been returning from Dartmouth. He met Miss Pitt near Kellerton Cross. They had talked no more than five minutes before Pinhay interrupted them with an insolent "How d'ye do, Sir!" He had not had his pants down; he had merely been readjusting his truss, having only just dismounted from his horse. His doctor had told him that should his truss ever come loose, he must set it right at once or his life might be in danger. The captain insisted that he had never had the slightest indecent familiarity with Miss Pitt. He had never even kissed her. When he learned that Miss Pitt had been sacked, he went directly to the rectory. Mrs. Fortescue asked that he leave immediately, "Miss Pitt doesn't want to see you, you've ruined her." He then discussed the confrontation with Rev. Fortescue and stated again that he had absolutely denied all the charges and assured the rector that Miss Pitt had nothing to answer for in her relationship with him. He insisted that Mrs. Fortescue had over-reacted to village gossip and the captain accused Mr. Fortescue of admitting as much, when he said, "You must excuse my wife." Delafosse said the clergyman remained adamant nonetheless that the rumour and scandal were enough to require Miss Pitt's departure. The rector then declined to apologise for any personal insult nor would he direct Mrs. Fortescue to recall her letters to Mrs. Willes. The clergyman announced that he was removing him as churchwarden and would henceforth refuse to administer the sacrament in St. Andrew's. When he was turned from the communion service on the next Sunday it was an intolerable public rebuke that Delafosse could not let stand. The Captain said he had brought this legal action with the complete acquiescence of Miss Pitt.

In his cross-examination, Mr. Crowder got directly to the point. By reputation, he suggested, the villagers had every right to think the worst of the captain's "walking out" with Miss Pitt. Did Captain Delafosse know a young woman by the name of Elizabeth Pidcock? He admitted that he knew her as a young woman in the village; she had a child of which he had always admitted paternity and he had paid her fully for her difficulties. "That was some time ago." The defense counsel mentioned the names of several other young women: Miss Palfrey (he admitted "I knew there were rumours that I was thick with her,") Eliza Ford, Elizabeth Steer and an ex-servant of his, Sarah Tucker. Delafosse, however, quite insistently parried all efforts to get him to admit to having seduced any of these other women. Answering one question, he shouted, "Well, if she had a child, it wasn't mine!"

The last witness was a Dr. William Hender. A Cornish physician, he was called to testify to having personally examined Miss Mary Ann Pitt and to have found the 27-year old woman to be *virgo intacta*. This opened a line of questioning on the part of Mr. Crowder that caused *The Times* correspondent to declare, "anything more disgusting in its details was never heard." In the words of the late Victorian giant of medical jurisprudence, Sir Alfred Swaine Taylor, the medico-legal subject of defloration is one upon which a great amount of "poetical discussion appears to me to have been wasted." He cites the case of *Delafosse v. Fortescue* in his *Manual of Medical Jurisprudence*. Taylor states that an unruptured hymen is presumptive but not *absolute* proof of virginity. That was known even in Crowder's day and Dr. Hender had to concede that point. As Dr. Taylor might also have pointed out, Captain Delafosse was a truss-wearing man of 64 years, many of them spent at sea: "In the case of an old man, or one of weak virile power, vulval intercourse might be had without destroying the membrane." Such possibilities, even in 1853, were not unknown to medical science. Further, it was not essential to show that the captain and Miss Pitt had consummated their passion for one another; the mere suggestion of such a dalliance between a married churchwarden and a rectory governess, and its patent notoriety in the village, was sufficient – in 1853 – for the latter's dismissal.

With such procreative and romantic matters having been thus frankly elucidated for the good jurymen of the West Country, it was time for the closing arguments to the jury. Mr. Butt, for Capt. Delafosse, suggested that the officer had brought this action, not so much on his own behalf, but more to rescue the reputation of a blameless young woman. There was no truth to any of the scurrilous village gossip. If the captain was the legendary village lothario that the defense had suggested, why had the Fortescues allowed him such easy access to their home and schoolroom? Nonetheless, the false charges against the captain and the innocent governess had been accepted and spread, first by Mrs. Fortescue and then by her reverend husband. Neither made any effort to check their facts. Mr. Crowder, for the Fortescues, reminded the jury of what they had heard from eyewitnesses. The rector and his wife had every reason to believe the truth of what they heard from Mr. Pitwood et al. Even the hint of scandal could not be tolerated in a clergyman's home. They had no other choice but to act as they did. It was the Captain's decision to bring this action that brought prominence to Miss Pitt's disgrace; Mrs. Fortescue had written privately, and quite properly, only to Miss Pitt's family.

Mr. Justice Erle left the jury to their task. It took some two hours before a verdict was brought in exonerating the Rev. and Mrs. Fortescue. The foreman said that they had concluded what the Fortescues had stated and written about the relationship between Capt. Delafosse and Miss Pitt was true and, hence, their actions were justified. The jury also ordered that Capt. Delafosse be billed for the costs of the Fortescue defense.

The Fortescues returned then in suitable triumph to East Allington having again established that the word of a Fortescue cannot be doubted or, worse, tested in court. The children were, presumably, delighted to see their mum and dad, having been left in the care of a new and, again, presumably, more virtuous governess.

In 1861, Miss Pitt – listed in the census as unmarried – was a school-mistress in Sheepstor, Devon, living still with her sister's family.

As for Captain Delafosse, mocked in the press as "a venerable Don Juan," it was obvious to all that he could not remain in the village. Nor did he. Even before the trial, he gladly left the prying eyes of Pinwoods and Pinhays and their ilk and had taken rented lodgings in Kingsteignton. By May, only two months after the trial, the naval officer was in bankruptcy court. He pleaded for relief from the legal debt owed to the Fortescues (over £270.) The Fortescues settled for an arrangement of payments of £20 per year. The Captain and his wife eventually relocated to a new villa in Wolborough, (then) a small village on the outskirts of Newton Abbot. Capt. E.H. Delafosse died there in 1870 at the age of 81.

The Rev. Henry Raymundo Fortescue would remain the rector of St. Andrews for another forty plus years until his death in 1898. The east window of the church is now dedicated to Mrs. Fortescue. It is among the newest of the Fortescue memorials that crowd the village church in East Allington.

Caught Off Guard on the Common

The Rev Herbert O. Francis, Curate of Great Torrington

THE NORTH DEVON town of Great Torrington has been quite accurately described as "pleasantly seated on a bold eminence." The town sits on a bluff, high above the east bank of the meandering river Torridge. The late Victorian visitor, John Lloyd Warner Page, who had intrepidly followed the Torridge from its origins on the Devon moors, approached the town from the east. He saw above him, "On the top of a declivity, rising mountainous from the river, and covered with heather, gorse and bracken, the town of [Great] Torrington. It is a grand view." [*The Rivers of Devon from Source to Sea* (1893)]

The views from the town itself are equally rewarding. From Castle Hill, the eye can follow the winding wooded banks of the Torridge and its feeder streams as they snake in all directions, making their way through the rolling fields and farms of Devon. A delightful and much used bowling green is all that's left of the old Castle. Nearby, an obelisk paid for by "the ladies of Torrington" celebrates Wellington's great victory at Waterloo. From the top of the town, the chimney smoke can be seen rising from tiny nearby villages with twee names like Frithelstock, Weare Giffard and St.

Giles-in-the-Wood. Just below the hill, the town is surrounded on three sides by hundreds of acres of green space, the celebrated Great Torrington Common. In the late summer of 1879 the common was the setting for a scandal involving a married curate and the daughter of one Torrington's leading citizens.

The Rev. Herbert Oldfield Francis arrived in Great Torrington in 1876. He was the son of the late Charles Larkin Francis, Esq., a cement manufacturer with homes in London and the Isle of Wight. Charles Francis & Sons were suppliers to those who (literally) built the British Empire worldwide. Herbert opted not to follow the other "sons" into the business and took holy orders instead after leaving Emmanuel College, Cambridge in 1862. He served the first six years of his clerical career in Dorset, first in the village of Canford Magna, then to Weymouth and later to Bradpole, staying the quite typical two years in each place. In the last of the villages, he met and married Mary Broadley Symes, the youngest daughter of a doctor from the nearby town of Bridport.

Married life for the Rev. and Mrs. Francis would begin in a place very far from the fetes and frills of the country parish where they met. The curate had accepted a posting at a church in Chatham located hard by the famous docks along the Medway. For the next eight years, the clergyman would work at St. Mary's church among the sailors and stevedores of the busy port community. His family was growing as three children were born in the early 1870's. It was probably an easy decision for the Rev. Mr. Francis in 1876 to take his young family away from the noise and stench of the docks and head west again, to the bracing air and open country of North Devon. He had been hired to be a curate for the longtime vicar of Great Torrington, the Rev. Samuel Buckland.

The parish church of St. Michael's, Great Torrington, has an interesting history. One of the early vicars was the later Cardinal Thomas Wolsey. In the 17th century, the Roundhead army drove the last of the Royalist forces down out of Great Torrington and harried them all the way to Cornwall. Before leaving the town, they blew up the Royalists abandoned powder supplies (and some luckless Royalist prisoners) that had been stored in the church basement. It had taken more than two centuries to repair the damage and the Rev. Mr. Buckland had presided over the final years of restoration. In 1879, Torrington was a populous town of almost 35-hundred people. In addition to being the local market town, Torrington's woolen and glove-making trades were then thriving and employed hundreds of townspeople. For Mr. Francis, he would be expected to assist with the weekly services at St. Michael's and handle some of the required parish visits. Additionally, the curate took on some of the public duties of the day. He was made the chaplain of the Torrington workhouse that "had accommodation for 250 paupers but seldom had a population of more than 180." In whatever free time he had remaining, the clergyman and his wife and family could take their rambles across the common and beyond.

On Monday, the 18th of August 1879, the clergyman took the advantage of a bright summer's morning for a walk on Torrington Common. He was unaccompanied on this occasion. On his walk, however, he had the pleasure to encounter Miss Lucy Beatrice Jones. The two were quite well acquainted, as Lucy's father was Dr. Charles Richard Jones of Castle House, Castle Street, and the chief medical officer of the workhouse where, of course, the physician worked closely with the chaplain. It will also be recalled that the Rev. Francis' wife was herself a medico's daughter so the two families had much in common and had become very close. Lucy Jones was 27 and she was not married.

Ordinarily, there would be no cause for any comment to be made about a married clergyman meeting an unmarried woman taking the air on the common; it was, of course, the preferred retreat for Torrington folk of all classes. The gentleman and lady might pause to share their thoughts on the dullness of the day, the recent weekend, and perhaps even the dashed Zulus, whatever. It should be here noted, for those not familiar with the setting for this encounter, that Great Torrington Common covered – and covers still – some 365 acres. It is rolling terrain in many places. This meeting between Mr. Francis and Miss Jones would take place in an area that would be later described as "a hollow or a gully." Their conversation, on any variety of possible topics, was a brief one, something between five and fifteen minutes. In the brightness of nearly midday, Miss Jones put up her umbrella for protection from the sun. For a married clergyman to have a private conversation with a young woman in a "hollow or a gully" was perhaps unwise. More so, since their friendship had already given cause for comment in some quarters in the town. To risk anything more intimate would have been recklessly daring. Who knows who might be watching? And there was an observer that August Monday and he would claim he had "seen all."

William Balkwill was also on Torrington Common that day. William was a 27-year old labourer from the town and a married man with no apparent record as a troublesome sort. While out on the common "hoeing turnips," he had espied the clergyman and Miss Jones together in a way that drew his peculiar attention and, leaving his turnips, he decided to settle in to watch. No doubt, he knew the two persons under his observation for his home on Mill Street was very near both the church and Castle Street, home of the Jones family. Seeing the clergyman move off at last and begin his walk back to Torrington, Balkwill emerged to approach Miss Jones. A remark that he made to the young woman, no doubt of a coarse nature, upset her very much and she cried out for the Rev. Mr. Francis to return. The curate hastened back to the scene and confronted Balkwill, insisting that the intruder's salacious assumptions of what had taken place on the common were wholly mistaken. Balkwill, in his turn, stuck to his story and suggested that it would be a tale of some interest to many people in Torrington. It was then that the Rev. Mr. Francis made the offer of a half-crown (2 shillings, sixpence) to buy Balkwill's silence. The cheeky man said the young woman's reputation would be worth more than that, for sure. He demanded a half-sovereign (10 shillings). The curate explained that he didn't carry that kind of money around with him and he would have to go home to get it and he arranged to meet Balkwill that afternoon with the half-sovereign. The transaction was completed later that day.

There was a fourth person near that hollow on the common. A Mr. Jackson, who came upon the scene only after the clergyman and Miss Jones had separated but he did manage to overhear Balkwill's remarks to the young woman. Jackson went directly to Dr. Jones to report that his daughter had been grossly insulted on the common. Things were soon to be spinning beyond the Rev. Mr. Francis' ability to keep them quiet. The curate was tormented by what had happened and regretted keenly his decision to pay the wretched man his money. Presumably, he told his wife first. Then, he went to the vicar, the Rev. Buckland. He swore that there was no truth to the blackguard's story; that he and Miss Jones had met on the common that day by chance and had only a brief conversation as friends. He had not been seated with her. He had never touched her. Shamefacedly, however, he admitted that he had paid Balkwill to forestall the man's threats to spread a false tale in the town. He had acted out of shock and weakness. He was stunned by the suddenness of the man's appearance as if from nowhere and greatly offended by his insinuations. In short, he had panicked.

The Rev. Buckland, who had been the vicar of St. Michael's for thirty years, knew his town and his parish. No doubt, he was aware of the gossip surrounding his curate's interest in Miss Jones. Unchecked, whispered over tea or over a pint and a pipe at *The Black Lion*, such talk would be very damaging to the reputation and efficacy of his curate and, by reflection, his own ministry. Dr. Jones, as well, was not at all pleased, despite the Rev. Francis' protestations of innocence in his conduct with Miss Lucy. All of this had to be ended. The vicar, Dr. Jones and even the Bishop's office from Exeter were, in the end, all agreed. Charges must be brought against William Balkwill for "making a threat with the purpose of extorting money."

The case was called on 24 September 1879, at the Great Torrington Petty Sessions, held in the Guildhall. The magistrates present were the Mayor, Henry Mallett, a High Street draper, and his predecessor, John Balsdon, a farmer. William Balkwill was then formally charged with "threatening to publish certain false libels touching and concerning the Rev. Herbert Oldfield Francis with the intent then and there to extort money from him." The courtroom was "crowded to its utmost capacity," reported *The North Devon Journal*; the onlookers drawn to see if the curate would be able to explain "in open court the rumours which have been in circulation for a month past respecting his relations with a lady of this town." Mayor Mallet warned that no outbursts would be tolerated. In the audience sat the vicar, Rev. Buckland, and the curate's wife, Mrs. Mary Francis.

John Thorne, a solicitor from Barnstaple, had the task of representing the Rev. Mr. Francis, the prosecutor of the charge. Thorne told the magistrates what they certainly already knew – this was a case of the gravest importance to the reputation of the clergyman who stood before them. A married man, with a fourth child only just born in Torrington, Mr. Francis possessed an outstanding reputation in the town and with his church. Unfortunately, over the past weeks, the curate had been the subject of gossip and rumour, and gross exaggerations about his conduct. Thorne had hoped that the magistrates would not be swayed by the talk "out of doors" and they had come into court with open minds. On the 18th of August, Mr. Francis, while walking on the common, had by the "merest of chances," met Miss Lucy Jones, a young woman of his acquaintance and friendship and a woman of an outstanding family and reputation. Without any planning on their part, they stopped in a hollow or depressed area to converse for a very brief period, something between five and seven minutes, perhaps. The curate took his leave and was making his way back to Torrington when he heard Miss Jones call to him. As Mr. Francis had walked away that Monday, he had seen Balkwill lurking in the area but had thought nothing of it. The man then made wild charges of what he thought he had seen and demanded money for his silence. Thorne suggested to the magistrates that if Balkwill had any complaint about the curate's conduct, why did he not bring those concerns to the proper quarter? Why, instead, did he threaten Miss Jones and Mr. Francis? He wanted to extort money from them. Anyone who would do that, said

Thorne, was "an enemy to society," worse than a thief. However, Thorne admitted to the magistrates that, regrettably, his client had agreed to pay the man. It was an injudicious act, Thorne stated, that was influenced solely by the alarm that the Rev. Francis felt at this sudden intrusion and the disgusting threats that he had received. He had also acted to protect an innocent woman's reputation. The curate had "promptly" reported all this to his vicar and it was the respected Mr. Buckland's opinion that this charge must be brought. The Rev. Mr. Francis had nothing to fear and came before the magistrates to clear his name.

The Rev. Herbert Oldfield Francis took the stand to recount the events of that day some five weeks previous. He was walking from the railway station, located on the river Torridge, some distance northwest of the town. He was walking back along one of the main paths across the common. There was cricket being played and he had taken a looping route around their game. Only then did he see, from a distance, Miss Jones who was then walking near the cemetery. He then veered from the path to the left and crossed the common to speak with her. They met in a dip or a hollow but not out of sight of the cricket players and others on the common. After a conversation of not very much more than five minutes, he had taken his leave when he first saw Balkwill "creeping around on his hands." At first, he paid him no mind but he had not gotten very much farther on his way when Miss Jones called him back. Miss Jones told him, "This man has grossly insulted me." He sent her away and confronted Balkwill alone. The curate told the magistrates that he had been totally taken aback by Balkwill's claims. The man said he had been watching them for half an hour, a claim that was simply not true. Balkwill stated that he had seen the two of them seated on the ground with the curate's arm around her waist. The curate insisted again that none of this was true. Balkwill told him that he had once seen a "gentleman behind a hedge" and that man had given him money to tell no one. The curate testified that Balkwill vowed he would let all Torrington know what he had seen unless the Rev. Francis "acted the gentleman" and paid him money to preserve the lady's reputation.

Mr. Francis said the suddenness of it all caught him completely off-guard and he agreed to pay Balkwill. They quarreled over the amount and Francis agreed to meet Balkwill that afternoon in Rack Park with the half-sovereign. He almost immediately regretted that action for he realized the impression that it had created. However, he wished to swear to the magistrates that Balkwill's story is "quite untrue. I swear there is not the smallest foundation for the suggestion that I was behaving improperly." Again, he explained that he had been "thrown off my guard as anyone would have been."

Another lawyer from Barnstaple had come down to Great Torrington to defend William Balkwill. Incledon Bencraft rose to question the Rev. Francis. Why was the curate on the common that day? He was coming from the railway station. Had he just arrived by train? The curate said that he had not but he had gone to the station to see about the schedule for a future excursion train. He had testified that when he first saw Miss Jones that day, she was by the cemetery, a very public area. Why, then, did they eventually contrive to meet for their conversation in the "hollow?" Mr. Francis said that was where their paths happened to intersect. Bencraft was interested in the curate's earlier testimony that Balkwill had accused him of having his arm around the waist of Miss Jones. Mr. Francis had never mentioned that before. The curate said it had only just come back to him. Bencraft asked, "Do you think there is anything else about that day that has come back to you, by and by?" The question drew laughter from the courtroom and a warning from the magistrates against any such "ebullitions of feeling." Mr. Francis was then asked the obvious question: if he had done nothing wrong, why had he paid Balkwill? Francis said, at the time, he was in a "state of bewilderment." The curate defended his actions, "Perhaps you have never had a threat of this sort made to you." Adding, as he glanced around the crowded Guildhall, "Nor any other gentleman here."

The Rev. Francis admitted that rumours of his relationship with Miss Jones antedated the commons clash with Balkwill. Wasn't his conduct with Miss Jones the general subject of gossip in Torrington? The curate would not comment on such talk but insisted that his friendship with Lucy Jones was a proper one that was known to all who mattered to him. Rev. Francis conceded that he had known Miss Jones for the three years he had been in Great Torrington. In addition to his friendship with her father, the curate had known her as a valued church worker. He had never met her on the common previously. He did, the curate admitted, on one occasion, take a journey with her by train to Exeter. They went to an agricultural show. Neither his wife nor any members of her family accompanied them but the train and the city was quite crowded.

Mr. Thorne was permitted to ask a few more questions of his client, following Bencraft. Rev. Francis said that Miss Jones had often been a guest in his home and she had most often come purposely to visit his wife. On the day of the rail journey to Exeter, while he and Miss Jones took the same train from Torrington, they had returned separately, several hours apart.

The next witness was Miss Lucy Jones, a woman – according to *The North Devon Herald*, "of some personal attractions who gave her evidence with admirable clearness and a good deal of spirit." She told Mr. Thorne that she had been walking that morning on the common, near the cemetery. As she continued her amble, by chance, she then met the approaching Mr. Francis. They were in a slight hollowed area but very much in view of the road to Furze Beam Hill. When Balkwill later emerged to confront her, he said "I seen all." She replied sharply to him that he had seen nothing. He said he knew who she was and who the gentleman was and it was a nice story he would have to tell. She then called out to Rev. Francis who immediately returned; at which point, she left. She denied ever being seated with Mr. Francis on that Monday. She had raised her small umbrella solely for protection from the sun and not as a shield. There were no improprieties on that day. There never had been any improper conduct on the part of the Rev. Mr. Francis. The journey they took to Exeter was entirely innocent, a gentleman had been in their carriage throughout the journey and she and the curate had separated soon after their arrival in the cathedral city.

Mr. Bencraft wanted Miss Jones to clarify what Balkwill had said to her that she found so "grossly insulting." He said he had "seen all." He said that he had watched her and the clergyman sitting together for fifteen minutes. She admitted that Balkwill had never said anything to her about the curate having his arms around her. Nonetheless, she found his manner and his comments insulting. Bencraft wondered if it was generally thought wicked in Torrington for two people to sit on the Common? Miss Jones said, of course, it was not wicked but she wanted to make it clear regardless that she had never been seated with Mr. Francis on that Monday morning. She had not gone there that day "expecting" to meet Mr. Francis. Bencraft suggested that it was then rather curious that Miss Jones and the clergyman managed to accidentally meet in such a low area? Lucy Jones said she couldn't help what unfriendly people might think. She was asked about the ferns in the area: weren't they quite high? She presumed not to have noticed the ferns. Bencraft asked if the hollow was very deep. Miss Jones recalled it as being "not very deep" for all that. Miss Jones was then released from the wiles of Incledon Bencraft and permitted to return to her seat. The prosecution then rested its case.

Mr. Bencraft told the magistrates that he did not plan to call any witnesses. He objected to the charge against Balkwill of "threatening to publish a libel." This was, if anything, a slander case. If sent on to the assizes, the courts would surely send it back. Regardless of the legal niceties, Bencraft suggested to the magistrates that they dismiss the matter out of hand. This was nothing but a "storm in a teapot." Such things will often happen: "Suppose a gentleman had transgressed by walking home with someone else and was in danger of getting a wigging from his wife … the most logical thing for a man to do was buy the chap a glass of beer or the like." This hardly rises to the crime of extortion. Bencraft maintained that it was the clergyman who first mentioned money. Not only did he agree to pay, but he agreed to pay more when his first offer was rejected. Rev. Francis had said he had been caught "off guard" by Balkwill's presence on the common. A strange phrase to use if the clergyman's conduct that day had been totally blameless. When was the curate able to get back "on guard?" If bewildered at first, he nonetheless quickly began to barter with the man over payment. Then he went off to get the half-sovereign and kept his word to meet Balkwill later that day. Was he still off-guard then? Did he use that interval of an hour or more for reflection or to go "promptly" to his vicar? Did he go to the police? No, he went to his home and got the requested half-sovereign. It seemed to be a very considered action taken on the curate's part.

Only three people – concluded Bencraft - really knew what had happened in the gully on Torrington Common on that recent Monday: the curate, Miss Jones and his client. William Balkwill, by law, could not testify. No matter thought, Bencraft, because in Torrington, nothing that could be said in the courtroom would lift the suspicion that still hung over the curate's conduct. The circumstances of this supposedly chance meeting between a clergyman and a young woman were certainly peculiar. There was no way to prove which of the two men was telling the truth. While certainly a clergyman should be credited for honesty, the word of William Balkwill was also worthy of some consideration. He was a married man of 27, employed on the railroad, his wife was a "gloveress" with a Torrington firm and he has young children. The Balkwill name was well known in the area. It is a censorious world, the solicitor reminded the magistrates. A clergyman should be like Caesar's wife, above suspicion. Bencraft said that could not possibly describe the conduct of Mr. Francis in this matter. This whole action was an attempt to "whitewash the clergyman at the expense of my unfortunate client and I trust that it shall fail." As Bencraft took his seat, *The North Devon Herald* reported that the magistrates were forced to silence the lustily expressed "manifestation of feelings" of many in the room.

The magisterial deliberations were brief. Mayor Mallett, prior to announcing the decision, cautioned those present that no demonstration of emotions would be tolerated. The mayor then declared that owing to the contradictory evidence, he and Mr. Balsdon both agreed that there was no prima facie case to send this matter on for trial. William Balkwill was ordered released. "A slight attempt at applause" was quickly gaveled to silence. *The Journal*'s correspondent observed that "from the demeanour of the public, it was easy enough to see the decision was one of which they approved." A public subscription was launched in Torrington to raise funds to cover Balkwill's legal bills.

In the end, it appears obvious that the Rev. Mr. Francis' decision to give money to William Balkwill, in whatever state of mind the clergyman might have been, had wholly compromised his insistence upon the innocence of his *tete-a-tete* with Miss Lucy Jones. If there was truly nothing going on but a happenstance chinwag between friends, then why did he not send Balkwill off with a defiant "be damned and go tell your lies?" On a much smaller stage, the curate's action is similar to the famous decision by Sir William Gordon Cumming to sign a pledge never to play cards again after he was suspected of cheating while at baccarat with the Prince of Wales. When the word inevitably got out, it was a little too late for Sir William to claim his innocence. His attackers had only to produce his signed pledge. In this case, the defenders of the Rev. Mr. Francis could never deny that Balkwill had his wretched half-sovereign.

The magistrates' decision to dismiss Balkwill left the townsfolk of Great Torrington free to place their own construction on the conduct of the Rev. Herbert Oldfield Francis. Plainly, from the "manifestations of feeling" heard in court, many had already formed the conclusion that he had, at the very least, placed himself in a most awkward position and embarrassed himself, his vicar and one of the town's leading families. In November of 1879, he was sacked as chaplain at the workhouse. When he appealed, a hearing was held by the workhouse board. The headline writers had now labeled it, *The Clerical Scandal at Torrington*. New witnesses came forward to relate observing the curate and Miss Jones "arranging flowers in the vestry" at odd hours. Something more was heard about the two having been seen "walking the sands together at Instow." Both the curate and Miss Lucy again haughtily rejected idle town gossip. Rev. Francis even had a letter of support from the Bishop of Exeter. It did him no good; the dismissal would stand. It was clear that he would have to leave Great Torrington. The Rev. J.F. Kempe, rector of the nearby village of Merton and prebendary of the Cathedral in Exeter, urged Mr. Francis to quit Torrington for his own sake and the peace and quiet of the village. In the end, Rev. Francis and his family did leave Devon but he would find it difficult to secure suitable new church employment. In 1881, he was living in Sussex at West Hoathly and employed as a chaplain to the railway navvies building the London, Brighton & South Coast Railway. In 1883, he was assisting at a church in Streatham. There, soon after the birth of another child, the Rev. Herbert Oldfield Francis died at the age of 45.

And what of Miss Lucy Beatrice Jones? The case certainly reflected as much upon her. It was indiscreet of her, as a single woman, to have been observed in a secluded area of the common with a married clergyman. Unlike the Rev. Mr. Francis, however, she couldn't be run out of town. Was she, at the age of 27, a wanton home-wrecker? If there is anything that suggests the innocence of this Francis-Jones relationship, it may have come in 1884. In that year, after five years of presumed public rehabilitation, Miss Lucy Jones married Rawlin Buckland, one of the vicar's sons.

William Balkwill went back to his job "packing" the rails. In the 1880's, there were concerns in Torrington about development encroaching on the traditional open space of the common. In 1889, the House of Commons formalized the status of the common and authorized the establishment of a Board of Conservators. One of the first nominees was William Balkwill. He continued to have an interest in whatever people were getting up to on Great Torrington Common.

Too Great a Coward

The Rev John Fitzgerald Nagle-Gilman
Vicar of Hennock

"THE ROAD to Hennock is an excellent specimen of the Devonshire Lane," wrote Mr. Murray in a late Victorian edition of his *Handbook for Travelers in Devonshire & Cornwall*. The lane is "frightfully steep in places, and so narrow, particularly where intruded upon by the boles of huge trees, as barely to afford room for the wains of the country." In December of 1875, the new vicar of Hennock made his way up that steep path to his new village. The Rev. John Fitzgerald Nagle-Gillman was accompanied by his wife.

This was Mr. Nagle Gillman's first vicarage after a peripatetic academic and church career. Born in County Cork, he was the son of Edward Gillman of Rock House near Bandon. Those were wild times in the Irish West and the elder Gillman fought at least one duel in 1823. After shots were exchanged, *The Connaught Journal* reported that "the business was amicably adjusted." John was born three years later and, like father like son, as we will see, he was not a man to suffer a slight in silence. His business would rarely be "amicably adjusted." He left Cork to take his studies at Trinity College, Dublin. Though *Crockford's Clerical Directory* records that he took a B.A. at Trinity and passed the Divinity Test in 1853, the official college archivist states, "This student does not appear to have proceeded to a degree at Trinity College Dublin as there is no entry under his name in the catalogue of graduates." Regardless, Mr. Nagle-Gillman did manage to be ordained in the diocese of Lichfield in 1856. He moved around incessantly, a fate not uncommon for curates without a patron, even more so perhaps for an Irish curate. He was briefly in Birmingham at St. Peter's. There was a stint on the continent as chaplain to the English-speaking community in Dusseldorf. Then, came a run of several curacies around London: St. John's in Fulham, the very fashionable church of St. Jude's in Chelsea, St. Matthew's in Bayswater and St. John the Divine in Richmond.

In 1875, he was pleased to receive the appointment to the open vicarage in Hennock from the Rev. Frederick Temple, the Bishop of Exeter. Though Hennock was hardly a posting that would have been much sought after, Nagle-Gillman was probably only one of dozens of hopeful curates eyeing the remote vicarage. Though remote, Hennock would not come cheaply. Such church livings had to be purchased. London based ecclesiastical agents traded and sold rectories and vicarages like estate agents. Most sellers cared little for the clerical hopeful's doctrinal soundness, if his finances were solid. And the buyers, in the most part, were more interested in the salubrity of the setting than any thought to their future sacred role in the village. One such ad prompted the humourists from *Punch* to crack:

> The views described with cool effrontery
> Are simply views across the country,
> And not religious views.

It is clear, then, that if Mr. Nagle-Gillman's years of wandering were ever going to end, he would need an infusion of capital. Happily for him, in 1873, he made, what was certainly considered at the time, if later events would prove quite the contrary, a very successful marriage. While he was serving as a curate in Richmond, John had made the acquaintance of Caroline Thomasine Christopher, the somewhat elderly and unmarried sister-in-law of the Rev. Alfred Millard William Christopher, the rector of St. Aldate's Church in Oxford. John was not exactly a young man either: on their wedding day, 14 May 1873, at the famous St. Giles church in the city of spires, John was 45, Caroline was 54. While we must always assume it was a love match for both, Mr. Nagle-Gillman could not have been unaware of that fact that his new relation by marriage, Mr. Christopher, was one of the day's leading evangelicals and an influential figure in Oxford and beyond. A word from the rectory of St. Aldate's would carry much weight in the campaign to find a place for the Rev. JF Nagle-Gillman. Of equal importance, the new bride's significant personal fortune could be tapped to purchase that long-awaited vicarage of his own.

And, so, the transaction was completed and in October 1875, it was off to Hennock. In the high waters of the river Teign, from the top of the "frighteningly steep" path, the village of Hennock affords extraordinary views of some "rich and delicious scenery." *The Palk Arms*, now and then the village local, still proclaims the view from their garden to be "the best in Devon." About fifteen miles southwest of Exeter, Hennock in the 1870's was a village of some 800 residents, many of them in the mining trade. The early years of the second half of the nineteenth century were good times in Hennock. "The upper part of the parish abounds in iron and a very productive lode is now in full work." Unfortunately, the new vicar would arrive soon after a typhoid outbreak that was blamed on impure drinking water had brought grief to many a cottage in the parish.

While the village may be "exceedingly picturesque," the parish church of Hennock is externally unprepossessing. A mostly 15th century structure, the church has been briefly described as "not large and rather low." Inside, on the other hand, a renovation was completed only shortly before Mr. Nagle-Gillman's arrival. The guidebooks inform visitors that the church can boast of one of the most beautiful rood screens in Devonshire. Directly across the road, stood the Nagle-Gillman's new vicarage with twenty acres of glebe at their disposal. It is a pretty picture.

Unfortunately, the Rev. Nagle-Gillman and his wife were not at all compatible and life at Hennock vicarage was most unpleasant. Mrs. Nagle-Gillman was soon writing to her sister and brother-in-law with her complaints of ill-treatment. Her friends in Oxford urged her to consider seeking a judicial separation and some preliminary steps were taken toward that end. Caroline's friends were then understandably more than a little surprised when the Rev. Mr. Nagle-Gillman presented a signed statement from his wife, authorizing her trustees to pay to him the sum of £2000 from her accounts. The request, coming as it did against the backdrop of Mrs. Nagle-Gillman's private correspondence, raised some questions among two of the trustees – the Rev. Mr. Christopher, and Canon Richard Watson Dixon, also from Oxford. The gentlemen wrote to Hennock and asked that the Rev. Nagle-Gilman permit them to personally interview his wife so as to allow them to hear in her words that she favoured this payout. If Mr. Nagle-Gillman refused to grant that interview, then the trustees would have to conclude that the vicar's wife had been the victim of a "systematic course of bullying or terrorism." From Hennock, Mr. Nagle-

Gillman insolently refused to make his wife available to the trustees and, instead, filed a chancery suit.

The Master of the Rolls, Sir George Jessel, was presiding when the case of *Nagle-Gillman v Christopher* was called in London on 14 November 1876. Mr. Frederick Waller QC was to speak on behalf of the Rev. Nagle-Gillman. He opened by admitting to Sir George that there was no gainsaying the fact that the marriage of the vicar of Hennock and his wife had been through a very difficult patch. Letters indicative of those unhappy times, having been turned over to the court, were no doubt written by Mrs. Nagle-Gillman to her sister and her husband and others. However, Waller insisted that these private matters were now no business of the trustees or the Court of Chancery. Counsel was very happy to report to the court and to the trustees that the Nagle-Gillmans were living in great harmony. It would then be even more unfortunate for the "painful details" of the couple's past disagreements to be dredged up again in a public forum. The document addressed to the trustees had been written in her hand and was under her signature. It was an indisputably valid exercise of her authority. Additional assurances of Mrs. Nagle-Gillman's determination to make this request had been provided to all the trustees. There was no legal basis for the trustees to withhold their approval.

The trustees were represented by Mr. Joseph Chitty QC, the leading practitioner in the Chancery bar, who earned the reported princely sum of £13,000 per year. As expected, Mr. Chitty presented to the Master of Rolls several of those aforementioned private letters that Mrs. Nagle-Gillman had written to the Christophers in Oxford. Chitty said the letters demonstrated an almost entirely variant picture of life at Hennock vicarage. There was no evidence of the "harmony" now said to exist between the vicar and his wife. Rather, Chitty suggested that the letters from Mrs. Nagle-Gillman, cited by her husband, in which she apologized for some of her earlier statements, bear "the impress of another hand." If there was no pressure placed upon his wife, then why did Mr. Nagle-Gillman persist in refusing to allow her to meet privately with her trustees. Instead, Chitty presented to the court the curt written response they had received from Mr. Nagle-Gillman:

> Mr. Nagle Gillman declines for himself and his wife to hold any communication with the Rev. AMW Christopher except through his solicitor, and when he and his accomplice hear finally through that channel he will probably think that he has heard too soon, his present host and hostess included.
> PS: The wicked are snared in their own net.

From the bench, the Master of the Rolls read aloud from some of Mrs. Nagle-Gillman's letters. *The Daily Telegraph* called them "some extraordinary extracts." Mrs. Nagle Gillman had written to Oxford claiming that her husband had warned her that if she did not obey his wishes, she would be guilty of disobeying the divine law that a wife must submit to the will of the husband. Because of her sinful actions, she would then forfeit her right to receive the sacraments, including the Eucharist. Sir George Jessel was of the Jewish faith. He declared, nonetheless, that he was forced to conclude from what he had read that Mrs. Nagle Gillman had been placed under "cruel pressure" to coerce her to agree to turn over £2000 to her husband. The Master of the Rolls admitted that his first impressions were most decidedly inimicable to the interests of the plaintiff, but Sir George cautioned himself, if no one else, that "indignation is not a luxury in which a judge can indulge." Rather than summarily dismiss the action, he would, instead, order a two-week adjournment. If Mr. Nagle-Gillman still wished to persist in his action, Sir George then advised him, he must agree to present his wife to be questioned publicly in the Court of Chancery. Sir George said that he would make no ruling in the case until he and the trustees, and the by now greatly interested public, all had a chance to hear from the wife of the vicar of Hennock.

A fortnight passed and the parties reassembled before Sir George Jessel. Mrs. Caroline Christopher Nagle-Gillman was indeed present on this second occasion, in the company of her husband. The vicar's attorney, Mr. Waller, immediately asked that the testimony of Mrs. Nagle-Gillman be taken *in camera*. He told Sir George that she was not a strong woman and a public ordeal might seriously endanger her health. Mr. Chitty for the trustees objected to the request and the Master of the Rolls said that he was forced to reject Mr. Waller's appeal. While the court had no wish to put Mrs. Nagle-Gillman through any unnecessary stress, such private testimony had been traditionally reserved only for cases involving lunacy, infancy or crimes of indecency.

The first witness to appear for Mr. Nagle Gillman was not, after all, his wife. John T. Campbell, "a senior partner in an eminent West End firm of solicitors" who had drafted the formal request from Mrs. Nagle-Gillman to the trustees, was called to attest to the document. He said it was completely straightforward and not at all unusual. He had drafted dozens of them. Mr. Chitty, on the other hand, won the admission from Campbell that he had never discussed the matter personally with Mrs. Nagle-Gillman. The vicar of Hennock had come to the solicitor to ask that the document be prepared for his wife's signature. Campbell insisted that that was not anything out of the ordinary; since Mr. and Mrs. Nagle-Gillman were living together as man and wife, a solicitor would have had no reason to challenge the gentleman's request. At no time had he ever suspected any irregularities in the proceedings and he would have declined the commission had he done so. Despite such a vigorous defense of his role in the case, before the hapless solicitor was allowed to step down, Sir George Jessel intervened "with great regret" to state that he thought that Campbell had shown a most unprofessional "want of caution."

The paperwork issue set aside, the focus now turned to Mrs. Nagle-Gillman who was called to the stand by her husband's counsel. *The Daily Telegraph* described her appearance as "nervous and distressed" throughout. Her responses were given in a very quiet voice. The wife of the vicar of Hennock swore that her decision to ask the trustees to release the £2000 from her fortune for her husband's use was completely voluntary on her part. She had "quite assented" to her husband's original request. He had told her that the money would be used for various church and charitable causes. Mr. Waller gently raised the subject of the previous unhappiness with her husband. She admitted that there had been difficulties in her marriage and she had written some letters to her brother that contained charges against Mr. Nagle-Gillman that she now wished to recant. Her husband had seen one of those letters and it had "exceedingly pained him." For some time, he was very angry with her but he then forgave her. She said that it was her wish to demonstrate her gratitude for his "kind treatment" that led her to approach the trustees for the money.

Mr. Chitty, very solicitously I'm sure, assured Mrs. Nagle-Gillman that he had no wish to prolong her ordeal in the witness box. Still, he said he must ask her some very important questions. The witness was not able to explain how her husband had gotten his hands on one of the letters she wrote to her brother-in-law. She admitted that she didn't generally keep copies of her letters. She then changed her story, somewhat, saying that he hadn't actually seen a letter but she had regretted writing them and decided to make a "clean breast of it" to her husband. She told him all about the letters and what she had written about him and there was a row. She still insisted to Mr. Chitty, however, that when her husband forgave her, she was moved by his kindness. She then acceded to the request for the money and hoped that it would be accepted as a sort of reparation for her hurtful words. Sir George Jessel, here again, intervened. He asked Mrs. Nagle-Gillman if, at the time she wrote these extraordinary letters to the Rev. Mr. Christopher, did she believe that what she wrote was the truth about her husband? The witness said that, at that time, she did believe it.

At that point, Mrs. Nagle Gillman was allowed to leave the witness box. Mr. Waller informed the court that he was prepared to rest the case for the vicar of Hennock. It had been clearly shown, he argued to the bench, that the request submitted to the trustees was duly and properly drafted, it was a routine request, and as the last witness had plainly stated that, it was her freely expressed wish that it be carried out. The announcement from Mr. Waller had caused an understandable stir in the courtroom as it had been anticipated that the Rev. Mr. Nagle-Gillman would follow his wife into the box.

Mr. Chitty quickly rose in protest, suggesting that the plaintiff "had not behaved at all like a man." He had put his obviously distressed wife through the ordeal of testimony and cross-examination, yet he shied from the same responsibility for himself. Chitty suggested that Mrs. Nagle-Gillman had had nothing whatsoever to do with the drafting of this request to her trustees, other than to sign it. The story she told of it being an act of reparation does not hold up against the letters she had written which detailed how she was the victim of a system of bullying, made worse by its appeal to spiritual intimidation. In her efforts to change her story to somehow make her husband's account seem more credible, she only revealed herself, sadly, to be a very weak woman subject to the vindictive influence of her husband. The trustees were well within their rights to refuse her request to release the money.

Sir George Jessel, after only the briefest consideration, delivered his opinion, which, to no one's great surprise, was to support the action of the trustees. The Master of the Rolls declared:

> A more scandalous and painful case has seldom come before me … This husband, who it was regretted, was a clergyman of the Church of England had thought it right to refuse the most cherished consolation of his Church to his wife unless she would act according to his wishes. That is the statement given by her, and she has sworn that it was true, and he, knowing the accusation against him, had not dared to go into the witness box to contradict it.

Sir George expressed his greatest sympathy for Mrs. Nagle-Gillman:

> Nothing could have been more painful than the spectacle of that unfortunate lady when giving her evidence today … her demeanour in the witness box showed that she was a lady

easily frightened. She was a person in that mental condition who could be compelled to say that she did something voluntarily. I have not the slightest doubt on the evidence of her own letters that the permission was obtained from her by an abuse of that authority which law and nature gave to her husband.

Her compliance to her husband's wishes had been "wrung from her out of fear." The Rev. Mr. Nagle Gillman's conduct could only be called shameful:

> I regret that anyone calling himself a man should have allowed himself to use the terrible power which his holy profession had put into his hands to wrest from his wife this pitiful sum ... I am not surprised that the person who had the heart to oppress a lonely woman in the silence of a private room had shown himself too great a coward to stand up in an open court.

So despicable did he view Mr. Nagle-Gillman's treatment of his wife, the Master of the Rolls said that he had been briefly tempted to rule in the man's favour, fearing that to do otherwise would expose the woman to even greater torment at home. "[I] almost wish that I could accede to the plaintiff's wishes but judicial duty forbids me to do so." He concluded with the official ruling that the submission to the trustees had been improperly obtained and, hence, could not be enforced.

The ruling by the Master of the Rolls was widely praised. *The Daily Telegraph*, which followed the case quite closely, said the Rev. Mr. Nagle Gillman had subjected his wife to a "long course of wretched and petty tyranny." The additional action of threatening to withhold the sacraments from his wife was nothing less than "abominable moral terrorism." All hail Sir George Jessel:

> It may seem like irony, especially for those people who have read *Bleak House*, to speak of the Court of Chancery as if it were a refuge and a tower of defense for the oppressed. It is however clear that a Chancery Judge has the power to do justice in a somewhat high-handed manner upon the merits of the case rather than upon its technicalities; and that husbands, guardians, trustees and other persons who stand in a fiduciary position and put their trust to their own advantage are liable at any moment to be summarily and sternly dealt with.

Whatever fears Sir George Jessel may have had for the aftermath of his verdict would be lifted when Mrs. Nagle-Gillman separated from her husband shortly after the suit was heard. A suit for divorce on the grounds of cruelty was filed but withdrawn: "There were really grave doubts whether the fair suitor would have been permitted to sustain the particular charge of cruelty referred to." Finally, and "in consideration of some pecuniary terms," Caroline left Hennock and moved to Oxford where, in the 1881 census, she was living at 40 Pembroke Street, the address of the rectory of St. Aldate's. She resided there with her sister and the Rev. Christopher.

The Rev. Mr. Nagle Gillman was left, alone, in Hennock. This disappointment in marriage and money seems to have driven the clergyman quite off the rails. His health collapsed; parish duties were transferred to a curate. Mr. Nagle-Gillman was afforded a medical leave in 1880. He was not a man to sulk quietly in rustic Devon. He was planning his revenge. Beginning in 1882, posters appeared in various places around Oxford. The unsigned placards carried scurrilous charges against the Rev. Mr. Christopher. The rector of St. Aldate's, at first, thought it the wisest course to ignore the attacks. He knew, of course, who was most likely behind it. In early 1884, when the Rev. Mr. Nagle was arrested in the Oxford Union, off Cornmarket, attempting to put up new placards, action had to be taken. The Rev. Mr. Nagle-Gillman was charged with libel and taken into custody. In all, he spent three months in jail awaiting his trial at the assizes, to be held in Reading on 22 September 1884.

What were these "painful libels?" He made the charge that his wife had been – prior to her marriage – the lover of her sister's husband – the Rev. Christopher. The rambling and convoluted screed should be quoted in full.

It is right and time at length that this bad man should be exposed, that the deeds and character of his private life should be made public; that the people of Oxford should know what a consummate hypocrite they have amongst them. He is the betrayer of another man's wife. A relationship of a certain character existed between this man and a near connection of his own. Her husband discovers the fact, and forbids his visits to the house; but the culprit pursues his course. He then gets private letters conveyed to her, and for a considerable period a clandestine correspondence is carried on between them, until at length, after many efforts, he succeeded in seducing this poor misled woman, the victim of his craft and sin, to abscond from her husband and had her kept in confinement. This is some of the private life of this bad man; but even this, bad as it is, is not all. Proceedings are taken and, in order to screen himself, this bad man, this minister of religion does not shrink from perjury. There are sworn documents in the solicitor's hands at this moment which prove his perjury, and which may be seen by anyone. This is more of the private life of this bad man. Look at the miserable woebegone face of his poor downtrodden wife and does not this tell the tale of the private life of this most wicked man. There is much more to be told, but enough. Let the people know what kind of man they have amongst them; one of the loudest professors of religion and holiness in the country but in truth one of the most consummate scoundrels and craftiest villains in the secrecies of private deeds. Observe him. Did ever honest man have that leering eye, and that canting voice of assumed sanctity? Let every honest man shun and expel him. It is now said that he has the hardiness to take this wretched woman into his own house, his miserable wife consenting, in order to screen her nearest relative and hood-wink the public now the rumours are about, and both are growing old. The facts here referred to are of old date. In early life he paid his addresses to her, but marriage was not permitted on account of her extreme youth; he then turned around and married her elder sister, but he has ever held a pernicious influence over her, at times most guilty. The thing has always been known as a secret in the family. One fearful outcome of the whole has to bring ruin on the domestic peace of the pure-minded man who married her, being ignorant of how things stood.

These were obviously charges of a "very serious character," declared the prosecutor, H.D. Greene, as he opened the proceedings. He insisted that Mr. Christopher, the victim of this malicious and false libel, had no wish to prosecute; but when his tormentor was arrested in the act of posting these libels in the heart of Oxford, he had been forced to act. No one who knew Mr. Christopher could believe that this venerable and respected clergyman could be guilty of the kinds of charges that had been made against him. On the stand, the Rev. Christopher swore there was not the slightest truth whatever to any charge that he had ever been guilty of any improprieties or impurity with Caroline Chistopher, now the estranged wife of the accused. After her separation from her husband, Caroline had been a welcome guest under Mr. Christopher's roof with his wife's full concurrence and approval.

Arthur Jelf QC defended the vicar of Hennock and freely admitted to the court that this was a very unfortunate story. The two clergymen had married two sisters. Mr. Nagle-Gillman's marriage had been an unhappy union from the outset and his wife had left him to return to Oxford where she now resided at St. Aldate's rectory. "Rightly or wrongly," said Jelf, the vicar of Hennock blamed his brother-in-law for the failure of his marriage.

> That was the strong impression upon his mind and that impression ripened and deepened until, with brooding upon his sorrows and troubles, thrown into a wretched state of health, during which he was obliged to leave his parish … he became practically unhinged.

The Rev. William McDonald, curate-in-charge in Hennock during Nagle-Gillman's leave of absence, testified that when he came to the village, the vicar had taken to bed for over a year and was all but paralyzed with depression. The Rev. Dr. Langley Pope testified that Nagle-Gillman was obsessed with the end of his marriage and once told him, "Dr. Pope, not a day passes but what I pray for her." Closing, Mr. Jelf said that his client, however tardily, now wished to state that the charges that had been made in the placards were entirely false and he was prepared to make a full admission of guilt.

The Rev. Mr. Christopher, for his part, graciously urged the court to have mercy on his tormentor. However, Mr. Justice Lopes, who had heard the case, was not so inclined. Lopes said that "a more wicked and scandalous libel was inconceivable." He could not bring himself to agree that the Oxford campaign was the act of an "unhinged" man – it appeared to have been a plot deliberately executed with the intention of inflicting the maximum damage on Mr. Christopher's reputation. Since the Rev. Nagle-Gillman had already been in jail for 3 months, and considering the victim's request for mercy, Justice Lopes said he could do no less than order the vicar of Hennock to sit another three months in the Oxford jail, without hard labour, and he was to be afforded that treatment granted to so-called first class misdemeanants.

Upon his release from jail, the Rev. Mr. Nagle-Gillman made his way west, taking that "frightfully steep lane" to Hennock where he remained the vicar until his death. That propensity for picking quarrels never quite left him. In 1894, he was once again in court after being charged with assault. He had disrupted a funeral procession that had come to St. Mary's churchyard. The vicar had given express orders that any bodies dressed for burial "by a certain local undertaker" would be turned away. There was the predictable fracas and the vicar was in the middle of it.

John Fitzgerald Nagle-Gillman died in 1900. His detested brother-in-law outlived him by five years. The Rev. Mr. Christopher is remembered in Oxford as "a beloved and saintly cleric" and a memorial East window was installed in his memory at St. Aldate's.

The Greatest Insult to the Other Sex

The Rev. Henry Luxmoore, Vicar of Barnstaple

WILLIAM GILPIN, who crisscrossed England in the early nineteenth century, writing up his *Observations*, was quite chuffed about Barnstaple: "In a word, Barnstaple is the pleasantest town we met with in the West of England." Barumites, as the locals are sometimes called in reference to the old Roman settlement of Barum, are justly proud of their town. It is, they boast, the metropolis of North Devon.

Barnstaple is an ancient place, said to have been "a burgh of note" at the time of the Conquest. The parish church of St. Peter & St. Paul is proud to aver that it has welcomed the faithful as far back as 1107. The current building – though oft "restored" - is mainly of 14th century construction. Most notable about the structure is the spire, which is frequently described as "curiously twisted." Pevsner, for variety or quite possibly just to show off, called it "idiosyncratically twisted." Typical is this entry from the 1880 edition of *The Tourist Guide to North Devon and the Exmoor District*:

> This tower is surmounted by a quaint spire of wood covered with lead, all askew, the result of the warping of the timbers southward by the solar heat. There are some good 17th Century monuments, but architecturally the church is of little interest.

Barumites would certainly object to such a dismissive opinion of their parish church, even if from someone as distinguished (if long forgotten) as Mr. R.N. Worth, "F.G.S., &c." The townsfolk would much rather cite the comments of Mr. Gilpin who, while conceding the exterior of St. Peter & St Paul's was "by no means handsome," declared that the interior was splendid. When Gilpin visited in 1831, the church had recently been redone and the observant visitor thought the work "does great credit to those who devised and executed its late alteration and enlargement." Welcome words of praise, indeed, for the new and young vicar of Barnstaple, the Rev. Henry Luxmoore.

The Luxmoores were a Devon family of long-standing. The name has had numerous variant spellings, the original probably being Loosemore. The change to Luxmoore may have been a bid to cover the traces and perhaps the scent of the West Country origin of their name. A loose (or a looze) was a pigsty of some sort.

The Rev. Henry Luxmoore had arrived as the new vicar of Barnstaple parish church in July of 1820. He was 26 and a clergyman's son; his father, the Rev. Coryndon Luxmoore, had been the longtime rector in the Devon village of Bridestowe. Henry, following numerous Luxmoores and Loosemores before him, had attended Blundell's School in Tiverton. There are five Loosemores and seven Luxmoores on the list of Old Blundellians. Henry then left his home county of Devon to earn an M.A. at St. John's College, Cambridge. St. Peter & St. Paul was his first church.

Barnstaple in the 1820's was undergoing great changes. The new lace industry was adding jobs. The population was growing, doubling since 1800. Construction was underway everywhere: erected in the decade were a new Guildhall, a pedestrianised shopping street, and even a new Borough Prison. Surrounded by all this activity, the new vicar of Barnstaple was also presented with the pressing need to restore his church. When Mr. Luxmoore arrived, the landmark spire was more than merely curious, it was particularly dangerous. A recent lightning strike had given rise to fear that it could come down at any moment. Inside, additional seating was needed to serve a growing number of worshippers. The Rev. Luxmoore presided over this restoration cum expansion, increasing the number of available seats to 1800. It was a rather large undertaking for such a young clergyman.

Of course, the parochial duties of the church could not be overlooked while the carpenters and stonemasons were crawling about everywhere. The Rev. Luxmoore had his other obligations, including visiting the sick and dying among his growing congregation. It was on one such visit, in

1825, that the young vicar met Miss Elizabeth Irwin, who was neither sick nor dying. Alas, however, she was an orphan. Her father had been a corn merchant who had died in 1814. Elizabeth and her three sisters had a "small maintenance but no fortune." Elizabeth occasionally worked as a schoolteacher. She had come to Barnstaple with her youngest sister Grace, among the many new arrivals seeking the sun and beauty of North Devon.

The young vicar was, apparently, much taken with Elizabeth, who was a year or two younger than he. A correspondence was opened. Soon, Mr. Luxmoore saw his way to bringing that conversation around to the subject of marriage. However, he had to make it plain that his income was insufficient to support a wife at that time, and his family expectations were uncertain. This was not at all an unusual predicament; as late as 1861, it was reported, "the incomes of much more than one half our clergy will not properly enable them to support families." But Mr. Luxmoore asked Elizabeth to please wait two years. To this, a delighted Elizabeth quickly agreed.

The young couple would, of course, see each other quite regularly. They would "walk out together," with Grace, the Irwin's youngest, as their attendant chaperone. There was much to do; the great Barnstaple fair in September, fetes and musicales (the local Musical Society was rated as "highly talented.") And, by crossing the Taw via the old Long Bridge, they could enjoy long walks into the delightful vale of Tawton, where Mr. Gilpin (perhaps, by now, a bit overheated in his *Observations*) found the view "carries the eye far and wide into its rich and ample bosom." The two years passed happily and, we may presume, quickly in Barnstaple. Too quickly, unfortunately, for Mr. Luxmoore confessed to Miss Irwin in 1827 that he was no more financially prepared to marry her then than previously. Between the ongoing demands on his time and purse with the restoration project and his own poverty, he was no more ready to take on the additional expense of a wife, much less a poor one, however attached he most ardently remained to her.

The patience of Miss Elizabeth Irwin must be ranked highly among her indisputable attributes. She understood his predicament completely and therefore expressed her willingness to wait upon his improving expectations. She even spent a brief time living on the continent, trusting that her faithful swain would be there upon her return. When she did come back to Barnstaple matters continued as before between them: the vicar escorting Elizabeth to the sermons, lectures, attractions and (suitable) gaieties of late-Georgian Devon. Such an open-ended engagement in hopes of someday finding the financial wherewithal to marry would not have surprised most

Victorians at all. In *David Copperfield*, Mr. Traddles – ironically engaged to a Devonshire clergyman's daughter, explained his situation thusly:

> I dare say ours is likely to be a rather long engagement, but our motto is "Wait and Hope!" We always say that, "Wait and Hope." We always say that. And she would wait, Copperfield, till she was sixty – any age you could mention – for me.

The years passed for Henry Luxmoore and Elizabeth Irwin. The 1830's arrived bringing with them the first Reform bill and William, the "Sailor King." The 1830's also brought home to England, from India, a young gentleman with the name of Beezley. He had formerly known the Irwin family and sought them out, tracing them to their new home in Barnstaple. While no doubt saddened to hear that the sisters had been left orphaned, Beezley began to pay his attentions to Miss Elizabeth. News of this development had soon reached Vicarage House and served to stir the embers of the perhaps failing ardor of the Rev. Luxmoore. Choosing a time when this intruder who had cast such a cloud over his prospect of domestic happiness was away, the vicar toddled off to the Irwins to assess the current lay of the land. Miss Elizabeth was touched by the clergyman's restated attentions and she assured him that young Beezley was no more than a family acquaintance. To settle any unease on Mr. Luxmoore's part, Elizabeth promptly agreed to dismiss this rival suitor. And, so, Beezley was sent away.

It was difficult to keep a secret in Barnstaple, as we have seen with Mr. Luxmoore's antennae picking up the timely news of bothersome Beezley. Such intelligence will, of course, pass both ways. Alas for Miss Irwin, her informers brought her the word too late. Her extreme distress can easily be understood when she was informed in February of 1837, that the Rev. Henry Luxmoore was engaged to be married. In London when the word reached her, Elizabeth hurried to Barnstaple to demand answers from the Rev. Luxmoore. In a letter, she called upon the vicar as "a man of honour and a gentleman, but above all as a servant of God, to recollect his promises to her." She received no response.

The details of the engagement, as they became clearer to Miss Irwin, must have been enormously painful for her. After her years of patient waiting, Elizabeth Irwin was now past her fortieth birthday. The vicar's bride-to-be was 29. Not only was the vicar's chosen future wife much younger than the shelved Miss Irwin - her family connections were also vastly superior. Miss Irwin's late father had been but "in trade." Mary

Jane Noble's father was an Admiral. Moreover, James Noble had been singled out by the great Lord Nelson himself, as one of the so-called "fine fellows" with Hardy, etc. Nelson had specifically praised Noble as one of those "whose merits and repeated wounds suffered in fighting the enemies of this country entitle him to every reward a grateful nation can bestow." Trafalgar having brought naval peace, and – sadly - Nelson's heroic death, Admiral Noble had then settled in Devon at Bishopsteignton. Mary Jane was one of ten children born to the first of the Admiral's three wives. Her marriage with the vicar of Barnstaple was arranged for 7 June 1838 at the groom's own church of St. Peter's. By the following spring, the new Mrs. Luxmoore was carrying the couple's first child.

This pretty picture of Devon society was to be muddled with the word that Miss Elizabeth Irwin had filed a breach-of-promise suit against the Rev. Luxmoore. In the words of her counsel, Miss Irwin was seeking compensation for "one of the greatest insults which it is in the power of a man to offer the other sex." It might seem surprising that Miss Irwin waited until a year after Mr. Luxmoore's marriage to bring her action against him. However, in her overview of the Victorian breach of promise trial, *Promises Broken*, Ginger Frost says such lengthy delays were quite common. Then, as now, lawyers for both sides would bluff and bluster in hopes of either intimidating the plaintiff to withdraw or cajoling the defendant to offer a pre-trial settlement. This pressure to settle was felt much more heavily by the defendant:

> Breach of promise was an action biased towards women, in part because it allowed them to construct their actions within a melodramatic setting. The plaintiff played the part of the victimized heroine and the judge and jury usually sympathized; indeed, judgments for the plaintiff, as long as she played the role properly, were almost automatic. (Frost)

Miss Irwin and the Rev. Luxmoore did not settle and her case was to be heard before James Scarlett, the first Lord Abinger, at the Western Assizes on 19 June 1839. Her counsel was Francis Valentine Lee; the Rev. Luxmoore was to be defended by Frederick Thesiger. The members of the jury were all men, of course, but presumably many of them were married and, of them, some were surely the fathers of presently or future eligible daughters. Mr. Lee would recount for them, in the highly emotional manner common to his brethren in such cases, the story of the thirteen-year acquaintance of his client with the vicar of Barnstaple. In 1825, Miss Irwin – a woman "eminent for her virtue, her beauty and her accomplishments," met the Rev. Luxmoore when he came to visit the sickbed of a mutual friend. Prior to that date, Miss Irwin and her sisters, in their bereavement following their father's death, had chosen to live a secluded life, "happily in their own society." However, soon after that first meeting, Mr. Luxmoore opened a correspondence with Elizabeth and it soon led to his decision to pledge to her "his heart and his future fortunes." When apprised of what her suitor had described as "peculiar obstacles" to his imminent prospects of attaining those aforementioned fortunes, Elizabeth happily agreed to wait upon her betrothed lover for at least two years. After two years, it was again agreed between them that it would be better to wait longer still than to marry without the needed income for a joint household that would perhaps be soon blessed with children. What Mr. Lee chose to describe as "this affectionate understanding" continued for several years. When Mr. Beezley came home from India and offered an alternative hand to Miss Irwin, she sent him away – at the specific inquiry and request of the Rev. Luxmoore.

And, now what was to be her reward for this constancy? To her "great dismay," she was to learn entirely by second-hand reports that her perfidious lover had engaged himself to a much younger and wealthier woman. A letter written by Miss Irwin – penned "in a tone and style creditable to the writer's understanding" – was sent to the Rev. Luxmoore expostulating on her disappointment and her betrayal. He replied to her in a "cool and heartless manner." Luxmoore, rather than come to her as a gentleman, sent an intermediary, with whom she refused to parlay. Finally, Luxmoore ashamedly came to her. She reminded him that he had pledged his heart and fortune to her. According to Lee, all Luxmoore could say to Miss Irwin was that he was "mad" and couldn't be held legally responsible for anything he had ever said or promised. The vicar added that he was a very poor man and if she had any thoughts of suing him, it would be a very costly procedure and she would get nothing from him.

"Thus, m'Lord, have this lady's feelings been trifled with," thundered Mr. Lee. It can be imagined that the counsel pointed his bony finger at the woman so desolate before them all. She now sat alone in the courtroom an abandoned woman, a spinster of 43. (Reports of Elizabeth's age vary: in the 1841 Census she gave her age as 40, making her 38 at the time of the trial. Had she overstated her age for legal effect?) Also, seated in the courtroom was her erstwhile betrothed, the newly wed vicar of Barnstaple parish church, married to a heroic Admiral's daughter and awaiting the birth of his first child. But what suitable gentleman would have Miss Irwin now? Worse, what might the scandal-mongering gossips of North Devon be saying had prompted the respected vicar of Barnstaple to break his pledge? What harm had already been done to her reputation? The counsel concluded his opening speech by indicating to the jury that this certainly is a case meriting significant compensation. Miss Irwin must receive the damages that will "restore her to that position in society from which she cannot but have fallen through the ill-treatment of the reverend defendant."

Lee spoke at some length perhaps to offset the fact that the evidence he had was so thin. There were some letters from the Rev. Luxmoore to Miss Irwin – a few even fit the description of love letters - but they were no proof of an engagement lasting beyond that first two-year window. As a witness, Miss Irwin had to admit that she had never been introduced to the Luxmoore family. Nor was she very often seen with the vicar in general Barnstaple society. She suggested that, owing to her limited means, she didn't get out much.

The only other witness to be called for the plaintiff's side was Grace Irwin. Elizabeth's younger sister had also remained unmarried. Grace said that she understood from the beginning that her sister and the vicar had been engaged. She testified to having been frequently in the company of her sister and the vicar as they "walked out together." The latter expression was fraught with implications for a single man and woman. As late as 1888, *The London News* remarked:

> The unwritten law would seem to be that after a tentative walk or two, if the couple still persists in selecting each other's companionship, the affair may be regarded as an engagement.

Grace concluded by stating she fully believed that her sister and the clergyman were engaged and until the day she learned of his betrayal, she had fully expected her sister would someday be the vicar's wife.

Not to say more than the truth, it was a tall task that awaited Mr. Thesiger. "Thin-faced, tall and graceful," Thesiger was said to prepare for the rigors of a day on his feet in front of judge and jury by each morning "committing to memory one or two of Spenser's stanzas." Presumably having done his memory exercise, Thesiger opened his speech on this occasion with a bold statement. He told the jury that, despite the touching appeal to sentiment presented by Miss Irwin's advocate, there had never been, in fact, any engagement, at any time, between Miss Irwin and the Rev. Mr. Luxmoore. While the vicar no doubt had found himself greatly attracted to Miss Irwin in 1825 and the subject of marriage had positively been discussed, all such discussions were had with the stated condition that any marriage was dependent upon "various circumstances well beyond the clergyman's control." It was absurd for two people without sufficient income to contemplate a marriage. The young couple had settled upon a two-year period in the hopes of something possibly turning up but it had not. Though Mr. Luxmoore had always maintained a "great inclination" towards Miss Irwin and the "warmest attachment" for her, it was no more than that. He had always agreed that if his feelings were ever to change, he would inform Miss Irwin. So he had. Thesiger told the jury that the Rev. Luxmoore was bound by no promise, in fact or in law, to marry the woman.

Before taking his seat, Thesiger said he wished to add a final comment at the specific request of his client. It was not unknown for a defendant in such cases to bring to bear suggestions impugning the character of his accuser. Had she been unfaithful to him? Had he discovered some personality flaw or disturbing habits or insanity in her family? Thesiger said the Rev Luxmoore wished to make it plain. If Miss Irwin had come into this court by way of restoring her character and reputation, Mr. Luxmoore was here in court to declare that, from the first meeting until this unhappy occasion, he had always had the greatest respect for Miss Irwin and considered her to possess, then and still, a "spotless reputation."

It was time now for Lord Abinger to instruct the jury. "Portly, full-faced and florid," with a patch over one eye, Lord Abinger had just turned seventy. He had perfected the air of studied indolence as an advocate and now a judge: "the chin of that ample face rested upon the still more ample chest as the motion of the lips alone would be enough for all that would have to be said." His Lordship said the jury must now decide whether there had been a promise made by the Rev. Mr. Luxmoore to marry Miss Irwin. Miss Irwin believed there was. Mr. Luxmoore insisted there was only a conditional offer. There was no direct proof. There was no signed letter. There was no ring. Not that there had to be; according to *How to Behave*, a contemporary etiquette book likely unknown to Lord Abinger, "The engaged need not take particular pains to explain the nature of the relation to which they stand with each other, nor should they attempt or desire to conceal it." Lord Abinger reminded them that Grace Irwin had testified that she believed her sister's engagement to Mr. Luxmoore had been quite established and she believed it to still be in effect up to the time of the defendant's engagement to Miss Noble. Finally, the jurors were asked to again review the letters in which the two disputants alluded to their affection for one another. His Lordship did indicate, however, that there was nothing written carrying any sense of a promise to marry.

If the jury found that a promise had existed and been breached, they then had absolute discretion in deciding how much the defendant could be mulcted for damages. In another Victorian case, Mr. Justice Willes said the jury must consider:

> Not merely the loss she sustained in not becoming the wife of a gentleman of property ... but she was also entitled to be compensated for the aggravation of that loss by reasons of her prospects of marrying another being materially lessened. I put this in the driest language I can select.

Rev. Mr. Luxmoore's annual income from the church was roughly £300.

The Devon jurymen were at their business for some little time before informing his Lordship that they had been unable to reach a verdict. Lord Abinger delivered the traditional admonition from the bench that the jurors need to go at it once again and those in the minority, especially, need rethink their findings. The jury returned to find that the Rev. Luxmoore had, in fact, breached his promise to marry Miss Elizabeth Irwin. For her damages, the jury found that the Rev. Luxmoore should pay the sum of £400. That should be considered a sizeable damage award for the time and considering Mr. Luxmoore's income. It must be presumed that Miss Noble had brought some wealth to the marriage and he would therefore be docked a bit of that to soothe the pangs of rejection suffered by Miss Irwin. According to one – of many available – calculations, the damages would amount to something near £18,000 in 21st century values. The losing attorney, Mr. Thesiger, survived the setback, becoming some years later, Attorney General and then Lord Chancellor, taking a peerage under the title of Lord Chelmsford.

Mr. Luxmoore was merely the first clergyman of the Victorian era to be sued for breach-of-promise to marry; by the end of the century, approximately two dozen clergymen had been taken into court. Presumably, many more had privately settled to avoid a public trial. It became a matter of general concern to Church leaders that so many young clergymen, without family wealth, were being forced into dangerously long engagements. This piece of fretful and anonymous analysis appeared in *Blackwood's Magazine* in 1856:

> One painful consequence of the present system is, the violation of the good old adage, "Happy's the wooing that's not long a-

doing!" The notorious evil of long engagements becomes, in this case, exaggerated to a painful degree ... The prospect of a living, certain though distant, appearing to justify the formation of such ties, engagements are formed in early life. The ratification of which seems ever near but never actually comes, till both parties have passed their meridian, and the fulfillment takes place, if it is thought worthwhile that it should take place at all, rather as a matter or course than because the parties really desire it.

For the Rev. Henry Luxmoore, the denouement of his relationship with Miss Irwin was, to be sure, embarrassing but hardly anything that would disqualify him from continuing to hold his church preferment. He remained the Vicar of Barnstaple and by the time of the 1851 census, he and Mrs. Luxmoore were raising a family of six children at the vicarage. His eldest son, Henry Elford Luxmoore, went to Eton where he later became a popular master. Eventually, and quite possibly through his son's influence, the Rev. Luxmoore left Barnstaple for a quieter church, ending his days as rector of the parish church in Great Everdon, a village in Northamptonshire. The church was under the patronage of "the Provost and Fellows of Eton." He died there in 1876 at the age of 82. Meanwhile, in Barnstaple, the controversial late-Victorian "restorer" G.G. Scott came to the church of St.'s Peter & Paul and basically erased all the Luxmoore additions from the 1820's. Not much remains but the Rev. Luxmoore's vicarage in the "delightfully quiet enclave" near the old church.

As for Miss Irwin, Elizabeth and her sister Grace settled in the nearby Heanton Punchardon. We can conclude with one happy final note. The marriage records indicate that in the spring of 1842, a woman named Elizabeth Irwin was married in Barnstaple.

Scandalously Disgusting & Obscene Letters

The Rev Frederick Moysey, Vicar of Sidmouth

Clergymen are very frequently in receipt of anonymous letters.
Some of these are agreeable enough. Some are very much the
other way.

London Society (1886)

JOHN BETJEMAN came to Sidmouth on one of his post-war tours in 1949
and he later told his BBC audience: "The climate is so dominant in
Sidmouth, you can almost touch it … If it were not for the sea, Sidmouth
would be tropic forest." On the channel, at the mouth of the tiny, and often
disrespected, river Sid, the town has evolved, owing to centuries of shifting
sands and seas, from a once busy fishing village to, what it has been for
some 200 plus years, "a watering place of distinction." Betjeman was
hardly alone in his praise of the Sidmouth climate, described elsewhere as
"remarkable for its purity and mildness."

Mr. Black, in his Victorian guide to Devonshire, thought Sidmouth to be
a "neat clean town in the shape of a Y, the stem pointing inland towards the
green heights." The old maps of the town do bear some debatable resem-
blance to Mr. Black's upside-down Y. If you go with the concept, where

the two arms of the Y meet, you will find the parish church. This is hardly the venue to resume the curious debate over whether the church was meant to be dedicated to St. Nicholas or to St. Giles. For years, it was the former. Then, nineteenth century antiquarians discovered evidence they thought definitively indicated that some 13th century manuscripts had been misread and it should have been St. Giles Church all along. In 1857, P.O. Hutchinson, one such advocate, wrote that it was "rather hard upon St. Giles that his honour had been so long upheld." To spare anyone's feelings – sanctified or secular – the church is generally now referred as the Church of St. Giles *AND* St. Nicholas.

For that is the Sidmouth way: temperate in climate and temperate in atmosphere. It is a quiet place, where one retreats to avoid controversy, however arcane. In a listing of British health resorts of the period, Sidmouth was praised for being "free of the barbarities of the modern tripper-frequented watering place." It made it an ideal setting for "convalescents, invalids, delicate children, adults of feeble constitution and the aged."

The summer of 1865 would have seen the boarding houses and villas of Sidmouth crowded with visitors. The pews of the church of St. Giles & St. Nicholas would have been filled with local parishioners and convalescing visitors on Sunday, the 13th of August. Those assembled were treated to "the startling and unexpected" news that the vicar, the Rev. Frederick Luttrel Moysey, was resigning.

The Rev. Mr. Moysey was 49 and had been the vicar of Sidmouth only since 1861. His family was an old West Country clan of doctors and clergyman. (One Dr. Moysey had his portrait painted by Gainsborough in lieu of payment for treating the artist's venereal disease.) The Rev. Moysey's father was Archdeacon of Bath and Prebendary of Wells Cathedral. At Oxford, young Frederick had rowed stroke for his school in the second ever University boat race in 1836. They lost. In 1839, he married Arabella Ward, niece to the Viscount Bangor. The Moyseys had nine children.

Prior to coming to Sidmouth, Moysey had spent his entire clerical life as vicar in the Somerset village of Combe St. Nicholas, near Ilminster. His years there had not been untroubled ones. In 1842, one of his female servants, "a good looking young woman named Jane Fowler," had died from the much discussed effects of "tight-lacing." In the early 1850's, Moysey found himself embroiled in lengthy and expensive litigation with a Belgian governess, Emilie D'Abrassart. He and his wife had sacked the woman on grounds that she had hidden from them, at the time of her employment, that she was not a good Protestant but rather an infidel or, worse, a Roman Catholic. Mlle. D'Abrassart sued that she was fired without the required notice and eventually won. Mr. Moysey wrote to *The Times of London*:

> Disappointed as I am in the result of an action which I defended, not for a paltry sum of money, but on high and conscientious principles, I have yet the gratification of feeling that I have done my duty.

The Rev. Mr. Moysey survived these occasional crises in Combe St. Nicholas and remained there until 1861 when he came to Devon and the much larger parish of Sidmouth. The annual income for the vicar of Sidmouth was considerable; the wealthy parish afforded their vicar a sum of nearly £500. With his growing family, he must have also appreciated the larger rectory that had recently been "elegantly-improved and beautified." The first few years in his new church and community passed uneventfully. It was in the summer months of 1864 that the trouble started for the vicar of Sidmouth. The first of the anonymous letters arrived at the vicarage for Mr. Moysey. Then another. And another. The author of the letters accused the vicar of the vilest offences.

As the quote from *London Society* at the head of this story indicates, anonymous letters were not an unusual problem for a clergyman of, for that matter, anyone in Victorian public life. The author of the essay offered a theory: "The principle of anonymity is one which has taken deep root in the shy, reserved, island-like British character." The Bishop of London would later boast that he never read an anonymous letter; they went directly into the fire. Whether Mr. Moysey burned them or not, at first, the vicar chose to ignore the letters, hoping his tormentor would lose interest. That strategy proved unavailing. Making the matter worse was the vicar's sense that the author of the letters was very likely a member of the congregation at the Church of St. Giles & St. Nicholas. The penmanship and the vocabulary indicated that the writer was an educated person. The Victorian church was not all teas and fetes. There were bitter fights between pastor and congregation over liturgy, vestments, candles, music, tithes, and more. Even in a quiet "watering place," the divisive questions of the day could split a congregation. Actual fistfights between clergy and church-wardens were not at all rare. Sidmouth, however, does not seem to have been a parish of great ferment. Nonetheless, the Rev. Moysey had concluded that the letters were coming from "a small band known to him very well, persons of superior education, whom he had to meet and shake by the hand about once a week, [and who] had continually annoyed him for one cause or another." Still, he could not prove it.

The news of the "poison pen" letters was not widely known in Sidmouth but there had been rumours. Nonetheless, when the vicar chose that Sunday, 13 August 1865, to announce his resignation, the leader-writer in *Lethaby's Sidmouth Journal* called the news "startling" and stated,

> Very rarely, we suppose, has such a thorough, universal and painful feeling been excited in a parish as by the announcements of that Sabbath morning.

With some hyperbole perhaps, the newspaper declared that nothing else was talked of in Sidmouth that following week. By Thursday, a group of loyal parishioners had prepared a statement of support for the Rev. Moysey:

> We, the undersigned inhabitants of Sidmouth and the neighbourhood, learn with regret that you have resigned the Living and intend to remove from this parish. As a Christian minister we feel that you have performed the duties as required by your position and have been fully mindful of the welfare of your parishioners. The poor will miss the sympathy and liberality of yourself and Mrs. Moysey, and all classes your courtesy and kind attention. It would be impossible for us to omit this opportunity of expressing our abhorrence at the low, mean, and cowardly system of anonymous attacks to which we understand you have for some time been subjected. We think that those who could have lent themselves to such base conduct are deserving only of contempt. Finally, we beg to offer yourself and Mrs. Moysey, and to all your family, our best wishes for your future happiness and prosperity.
>
> 17 August 1865

More than 200 people signed the statement, led by His Grace, the Duke of Buckinghamshire. Perhaps disappointed at the number of signatories to the statement, *The Journal* thought it politic to note that, "it would be unjust to infer that non-signers had any sympathy with slander."

The police had been of no use in identifying the sender of the letters, so a reward fund was hastily cobbled together:

£50 REWARD: Whereas during the last twelvemonth a large number of scandalously disgusting and obscene letters have been addressed, through the Post Office, to the Rev. F.L. Moysey, Vicar of Sidmouth, the above reward will be paid to any person who shall give information as shall lead to the discovery and prosecution of the writers of the aforesaid letters.
At the request of several respectable inhabitants of Sidmouth, I hereby offer the above reward.
(Signed) Gustavus Smith, Salcombe Mount near Sidmouth 19 August 1865.

The Sidmouth Journal hailed the reward and thought it might be just the ticket to unmask the guilty: "May they speedily be unearthed, and they would soon find Sidmouth too hot to hold them!" There was still no progress in the investigation.

Regardless, all of this was coming together rather late in the game for the Rev. Mr. Moysey. He appeared "deeply affected" by the delegation led by Major General Sir Henry Floyd that came to the vicarage to present a formal copy of the "We, the undersigned" pledge. The vicar accepted it solemnly. Mr. Moysey made clear to all that it was impossible for him to change his mind and his decision to resign was irrevocable. He told the small party of supporters that when he said he "knew" the source of the letters, he used the word in the sense that was generally understood. He knew but he could not prove it in a court of law. Now, it was too late; his health had broken under the strain of these attacks. *The Sidmouth Journal*'s correspondent quoted the clergyman as saying:

> The system of annoyance to which he had been subjected was unendurably painful, and that, in addition, the state of his health and that of his family, was such that should render it desirable that they should move to a drier and more bracing locality.

It does them credit, surely, that the Moysey supporters had not forgotten the vicar's large family. The local ladies thought that a small parting gift for Mrs. Moysey might bring her some comfort. She was presented with a "handsome ormolu flower stand, and a pair of candlesticks and letter-weight, all of burnished and ornamental gilt and electroplate." Whether some additional gewgaws for the Moyseys next home would be of any solace at such a time may be open to debate. However, Mrs. Moysey accepted the offering with her customary grace:

> My dear friends – It is impossible for me to express in adequate terms my feelings of gratitude for the present which you have made me at this moment, when I am leaving the parish. I accept it with thankfulness and shall never forget how kindly *almost* all the ladies of Sidmouth have come forward to cheer me when a few petty annoyances might for a moment have made me forget the honest and true affection of a large proportion of the parish. (Signed) Arabella Moysey
>
> 25 August 1865

The tumultuous Sidmouth month of August 1865 ended with the Rev. and Mrs. Moysey making a final series of "calls" upon the town's notables, "irrespective of rank or religious uniformity." The ever loyal reporter for *The Sidmouth Journal* thought the Moyseys could now take their leave from the town "convinced how hearty and general was the esteem in which they were held. That is the *only* solace we can now offer them, but their possession of it may help to lighten their otherwise painful load."

The duties at the Church of St. Giles & St. Nicholas had been deftly handed off to the Rev. H.G.J. Clements, who had been a curate in Sidmouth in the years immediately before the Moyseys arrived. *The Journal* hoped that the new vicar would be able to "steer clear of the dissensions and heartburnings which may be engendered by the circumstances which have again brought him to Sidmouth." To give the Rev. Mr. Clements his due, he remained the vicar of Sidmouth into the new century. The new shepherd of Sidmouth had apparently heeded the editor's advice:

> Let him but feel and act as the minister of all, and not of any party, section or clique, and he will not merely gain the esteem of all, but will find that esteem strengthen … but if aught like partisanship, undue sensitiveness, or a lack of confidence on either side be manifested, then it will be "good-bye" once more to peace in the parish, and Sidmouth will remain associated with the unenviable notoriety of being an ill-conditioned and quarrelsome place. For the honour of the town, let its inhabitants resolve that such a stigma shall not attach to it.

The Rev. Mr. Moysey and his family – meanwhile - relocated to London. The imperial capital would hardly seem to provide the bracing and dry climate that the erstwhile vicar had supposedly been seeking. Still, he and his wife remained at 91 Kensington Gardens until 1894 when, following the death of his unmarried older brother, the clergyman inherited Bathealton Court, near Wiveliscombe in Somerset. He died there in 1906 at the age of 90. A strange silence seems to have closed around the latter years of the Rev. Mr. Moysey. There was a brief obituary in *The Times* that made no mention of the Sidmouth scandal, merely noting that the Rev. Moysey had "retired in 1865." He never held another church living. The letter writer was never identified.

The Moyseys had left Sidmouth not two weeks after that "startling" Sunday morning announcement. It is unlikely, as their carriage pulled out of town, that they would have shared with John Betjeman the writer's parting thoughts, put down on paper eighty-four years later: "Sidmouth, silvery pink and creamy Sidmouth, sadly I say farewell!"

The Circumstances Are Somewhat Peculiar

The Mysterious Death at the Vicarage

The Rev. John Henry Napper Nevill, Vicar of Stoke Gabriel

The assumption of the medical character by a clergyman is, we firmly believe, rarely beneficial to himself or his parishioners.

THE LONDON LANCET (1858)

ACCORDING TO the Rev. Sabine Baring Gould, and to no one with greater authority on Devon could we turn than to the rector of Lewtrenchard, the village of Stoke Gabriel may be the prettiest in the county. "For loveliness of situation, Stoke Gabriel in a lap or creek, facing the sun, shut away from every wind, is the most perfect." The beautiful River Dart forms a three mile border for the village, which in the 1880's was among "the least visited and most primitive" anywhere in England.

The revered and Reverend Baring-Gould was not alone in his admiration for this place. Monsieur L. Valentin – in *Picturesque England: Its Landmarks and Haunts* – described the approach to the village by the river:

[Stoke Gabriel sits] in an amphitheatre of woods sloping to the stream, with the ivy covered tower of the Church of St. Gabriel, and the fishing cottages gathered around it. A very old and large yew tree stands in this churchyard.

Ah, yes, everyone mentioned the old yew. Another Victorian visitor to Stoke Gabriel, Henry John Whitfield, in his *Rambles in Devonshire with Tales & Poetry*, mused, "What a history, what a tale of romance might not that patriarch tell, could only that foliage, like the oak at Dodona, find a tongue!" So stirred by the scene and his racing emotions was Whitfield, he penned a rather lengthy ode, entitled *The Churchyard Yew*. A small excerpt shall thankfully suffice:

> Fairy spells, that memory weaves,
> > Shades with outline dim,
> Linger in thy whispering leaves,
> > Moan in every limb.
> Aged Yew, for many a day,
> > Wherefore dost thou murmur so?
> And the aged Yew replieth,
> > Well-a-day, well-a-day,
> 'Tis the ghost of Time that sigheth;
> > Life and death, 'tis mine to show,
> Life above, and death below.

Regardless of how one might receive Whitfield's poesy, it is surely true that the old yew had seen much. But, perhaps, nothing as strange ever took place beneath "thy whispering leaves" as the events of the 27th of January 1887, during the time the Irish born parson, the Rev. John Henry Napper Nevill was the vicar of Stoke Gabriel.

Born in 1848, the Rev. Nevill had been ordained in Armagh; after a few years in the Church of Ireland, he came across to England in the early 1870's. He had ministered in Beccles, Teddington, and Southampton before coming to Devon, first as curate at St. Matthias in Torquay. In 1881, he was presented with the vicarage in Stoke Gabriel. He was apparently a man of some out-sized personality; his views were strongly held, and his sermons earned him the title of "Fiery Parson Nevill." He was also handsome and unmarried. In Devon lore, it has been said that Elizabeth Durant, the unwed female owner of Sharpham House, across the Dart in Ashprington, had a window put in so she could especially espy on the Stoke Gabriel vicarage.

Village romance aside, more important to our story is the fact that, in addition to his divinity studies, Rev. Mr. Nevill had also found the time to take some instruction at Trinity College, Dublin, toward a medical career. In his clerical studies, Nevill may have stuck to the well-trodden path; in medicine, however, he early on strayed from orthodoxy and fell under the sway of Joseph Wallace, a gentleman who had coined for himself the title of physianthropist. Others with much less charity have called Wallace a quack.

Nevill studied with Wallace in London. He adopted the very strict dietary regimen that his mentor endorsed: an absolute ban on alcohol, tobacco, yeast, flesh meat, fish, salt and vinegar. He also mastered the mysteries of Wallace's twelve "specifics." Oskar Korshelt, in a way Wallace's tireless Boswell, said the specifics were "alcoholic tinctures" extracted from plants.

These specifics had the merit of being consumed and expelled by the patient naturally, eliminating "the secondary and evil affects, as is the case with all customary drugs." The Wallace specifics were numbered one through twelve and, depending upon the patient's complaint, the physianthropist could consult the chart and recommend the appropriate "specific." Korshelt and the proponents of "the Wallace cure" believed it was well past time that the power of curing was to be taken out of the hands of doctors and their poisons. "Even the uninitiated in the science of medicine may, without any scruples, cure themselves and their families of any illnesses which happen to attack them." Wallace was married to Chandos Leigh Hunt, a medium and faith healer, and the couple had as recently as 1885, published their treatise, *Physianthropy, or the Home Cure & Eradication of Disease*.

The Rev. John Henry Napper Nevill brought the Wallace cure with him to Stoke Gabriel. In this "most primitive" Devon community, it was not a skill to be lightly regarded. In addition to the vicar, residing in the village, there were seven farmers, four fishermen, two cowkeepers, two masons, a shoemaker, a tailor, two publicans, two shopkeepers, a painter, an Admiral (retired - more of him later), a Baroness, and two or three genteel widows. Please note that there was no doctor. The closest physician may have been in Totnes. There was no need for ailing residents to make that long walk any longer with the pastor having "the cure" to hand.

In 1886, a former housekeeper, Selina Laver, a woman only in her forties, fell gravely ill. Her husband, Henry, a sometime gardener at the vicarage, came with cap in hand, to ask if the Rev. Mr. Nevill might kindly try some of his "specifics" to save his wife. Selina, who had been living in

Southampton, came to Stoke Gabriel and was moved into the vicarage to be cared for by the Rev. Mr. Nevill.

Nurses were brought in from Torquay to tend to Mrs. Lever. All the medication, however, was prepared for the patient by the Rev. Mr. Nevill. At first, the poor woman rallied somewhat under the "specifics." Then came a turn for the worse and soon she was, more or less, unconscious. Joseph Wallace, the author of the "cure" came all the way from London at the request of his "student" for a consultation. It was thought advisable by the great man to make some very fine adjustments to the required specifics. Wallace pronounced himself satisfied with the changed regimen and returned to the capital; the Rev. Nevill, and faithful Henry, of course, remained in the vicarage. Selina Lever died on 18 January 1887. She was 46.

Under the laws of England, specifically, the *Births and Deaths Registration Act of 1874*, any death that might be thought unexpected, or having followed from some unknown cause or had given rise to any reasonable suspicion had to be referred to the coroner. No registration of the death would be permitted until the coroner had a chance to review the case and, if he thought it was required, to order a full inquest. The death of Mrs. Lever had excited a good deal of interest in the Dart valley, especially among those who had not signed on among the true believers in the efficacy of the Wallace cure. When the Rev. Nevill approached the registrar for a death certificate, the cleric was told that the coroner's office had been informed and it was thought necessary that there should be an autopsy on Mrs. Lever. The question of interment would have to wait.

The Rev. Nevill returned to Stoke Gabriel vicarage and determined for reasons he kept to himself that he would forego the niceties of paperwork. The vicar gave instructions to the church sexton, James Narracott, to inter Selina Lever in the churchyard. It was done and that would be that.

The vicar of Stoke Gabriel had not taken into account the feelings and powers of the formidable coroner for South Devon, Sidney Hacker. In all, Hacker held the post for forty years. Out of his offices in Market Street, Newton Abbot, Mr. Hacker was a solicitor, the commissioner for oaths and, by the way, the local representative for the West of England Insurance Company. Only two years previous, he had handled the famous "Babbacombe murder case." His forensics evidence led to the conviction of John Lee. It wasn't Hacker's fault that the hangman then botched the job, leading to Lee's legendary status as "The Man They Couldn't Hang."

On 27 January 1887, Mr. Hacker rode out to Stoke Gabriel for the purposes of picking a coroner's jury to look into the death of Mrs. Selina

Lever. The jury foreman was quickly chosen, the aforementioned Rear Admiral Richard Dawkins, JP was pleased to serve. His splendid home *Maisonette* was the showplace of the Dart valley. The preliminaries concluded, Hacker asked the registrar to submit the report on the autopsy on the late housekeeper. The registrar was forced to admit that no autopsy had been performed. At that point, Mr. Kellock, another Totnes solicitor, rose to announce that he had been employed to represent the absent Rev. Mr. Nevill. The vicar had instructed him to please inform Mr. Hacker that, with all due respect, save for a direct order from either the Home Secretary, Sir Henry Matthews, or the Bishop of Exeter, the Very Rev. Edward Bickersteth, he would not permit the body of Mrs. Lever to be disturbed.

As might have been imagined, Mr. Hacker did not receive this defiant news kindly. The coroner ordered the members of his jury, with a police constable as an escort, to march with him the short distance to Stoke Gabriel churchyard. There, in the gate, in the opposing forms of Coroner Hacker and Parson Nevill, state met church in a brief standoff. By now, a crowd had gathered. The onlookers made up in enthusiasm for their small number - perhaps no more than a dozen – but this was Stoke Gabriel. There was a brief struggle of some kind; accounts differ. One published report suggested that Mr. Hacker went over the churchyard wall. Another newspaperman reported that the coroner firmly "forced the gates." The "aged Yew" would know, as our friend Whitfield had told us, would that it could only talk.

Once inside the churchyard, Hacker ordered the sextons to unearth the coffin bearing the remains of Selina Lever. The Rev. Nevill could do nothing but stand aside. The grim process of exhumation proceeded and Mrs. Lever's body was taken to the church-house – or vestry. There the jury viewed the body of the woman, an unpleasant task, to be sure, as she had by then been dead over a week. A warmer than usual January made matters no better at all. Mr. Hacker and his jurors, with handkerchiefs to their faces, quickly took their exit while two surgeons, Drs. Davies and Haynes – were permitted to remove "certain organs" to be dispatched for analysis. Mr. Hacker adjourned the jury pending the return of those reports.

Exhumations were not entirely unusual in the day but few had been accompanied by such a personal showdown. The story of this churchyard clash was soon making national headlines. *The Daily Telegraph*'s readers were told, "the circumstances are somewhat peculiar." With the Rev. John Henry Napper Nevill having now been ordered by the coroner to attend the resumed inquest, it is no newspaper hyperbole to report that "considerable excitement prevailed" in Devon.

The Rev. Nevill duly presented himself two days later when the coroner's jury was once again in session. He testified that the deceased had been suffering from a chronic liver complaint and her chances of survival had never been great. He had treated her with a prescription recommended by a specialist who had made such disease his particular study. Rev. Mr. Nevill identified that gentleman as Joseph Wallace and he conceded that Mr. Wallace was not a licensed medical practitioner. Mrs. Lever had, at first responded to the regimen of specifics but in November 1886, her condition dramatically worsened and she was unconscious for most of her final days. The clergyman thought that these proceedings were completely uncalled for as he was able to state with certitude that the cause of death was liver disease. He should have routinely received the burial certificate he had sought from the registrar.

Henry Lever was called to testify after the vicar. He accepted the sympathies of the coroner and jurymen for his recent loss and the pain these proceedings must have caused him. Henry said he had freely requested that the Rev. Nevill treat his wife. The gardener said he had full confidence in the decisions made by the rector and his great friend from London, Mr. Wallace. During Wallace's emergency visit to Stoke Gabriel, Henry said that that gentleman had never presented himself as a doctor. Moreover, Henry said that he never felt a need to summon a doctor from Totnes or anywhere else. He had no regrets.

The two nurses from St. Raphael's Home in Torquay, a convalescent home for women, who had been with Mrs. Lever at various times until the end also testified. Both Alice Penzer and Isabel Paterson said that the dying woman was quite well cared for and that all the medications she had received had been prepared for her by the vicar himself. Nurse Paterson was on duty at the end. She testified that Mrs. Lever eyes had become greatly dilated and she went into a deep sleep. After being awakened to take her medicines, the patient vomited several times, went into convulsions and died around seven in the morning. Paterson went so far as to say – and be later rebuked for it in the medical journals - that she saw no need to call for a doctor because a doctor would have "done no good." A leader writer in *The Medical Press & Circular* reminded the young nurses that "it was perhaps no part of their duties to insist on a doctor being called, but they certainly held curious views as to the attributions and functions of 'trained nurses.'"

The next witness was Joseph Wallace himself. The physianthropist told the coroner that he had come the great distance to Stoke Gabriel in November to see Mrs. Lever at the wish of his good friend, the vicar. The woman was extremely weak and near death. He had diagnosed her as suffering from "chronic liver disease and a cancerous habit of the body generally." He prescribed two of his famous "specifics" intended to help the patient fight the disease that was slowly killing her. Wallace testified that the actual doses had been prepared by the Rev. Nevill, whom he had fully trained in that art. Wallace said he had then returned to London and was, of course, very distressed to learn subsequently that Mrs. Lever had, after all, succumbed to her disease. When asked by the coroner how he wished to identify himself, Wallace said he thought the most appropriate title would be that of "medical scientist." When Mr. Hacker asked if he had ever presented himself to Mr. Lever or to anyone in the village as a doctor, Wallace stiffened and replied, "Absolutely not. I may say, thank God, I am not a doctor."

The medical scientist was then excused and the next two witnesses were, in fact, quite willing to answer to the title of doctor. Dr. Lalonde John Cary Hains and Dr. Donald Fraser had examined the internal organs of the late Mrs. Lever. Dr Hains, speaking for his colleague, described the deceased's liver as being "very congested and friable." The lungs were also congested. The heart was healthy. The right kidney was friable. The left was fine. The stomach was empty but stained with some inky material. The stomach had been sent to London for further analysis and those results were not expected for some little while. The physicians did agree however that, in their opinion, the liver did not appear to be overly diseased. They also reported that they had found two rather large gallstones in the bile duct but they did not believe they had contributed to the woman's death.

The inquest into the "Devonshire Burial Scandal," as *The Times* had labeled it, concluded on 7 February 1887. The local poisons expert, Dr. Alexander Wynter Blyth, (who would also later help to establish the especial characteristics of Devonshire cream) had examined the stomach presented to him. He found that there was no evidence of wrongdoing, no signs of poison, and no evidence that any of the nostrums employed by the Rev. Mr. Nevill led to Mrs. Lever's death. She had, in fact, died of natural causes, i.e. cancer.

Coroner Hacker then recounted the case for his jury for better than an hour. They dutifully produced the verdict of "death from natural causes" and – no doubt to Hacker's great delight – added the statement that the vicar of Stoke Gabriel was very much to be censured for his failure to obey the burial laws of the realm. It must not happen again. Additionally, he was to be blamed for not seeking qualified medical assistance for his housekeeper. The hapless nurses were also to be chastened for not having made that recommendation. Let this, Mr. Hacker declared, be instructive to all the residents of Stoke Gabriel.

At last, the body of the late Selina Lever could now be legally interred near the yew tree in Stoke Gabriel churchyard to await the last trumpet. The Rev. Nevill devoted his next Sunday's sermon to the subject, telling his parishioners that he "could not but feel that a terrible desecration of holy ground had been committed but I, at least, am thankful that I had nothing do with that desecration."

For the Rev. Mr. Nevill, however, there would be no imminent peace. The medical press strongly condemned him for trespassing on their patch. This case in a remote Devon village was not without precedent. In 1883, a vicar in Kent, who had taken "occasional courses" at St. Thomas' Hospital in London, made up a tonic for a sick girl in his parish. She died within minutes from prussic acid poisoning. In 1863, a Rev. Hugh Reed claimed to have a found a cure for cancer; a claim that attained "dangerous prominence" after a write-up in *The Times of London*. When a Devon clergyman patient of the Rev. Reed's, who had publicly hailed the treatment, died from a painful mouth cancer, talk of the Reed "cure" subsided. As far back as 1858, *The Lancet* had declared:

> On the whole, we are disposed to think that it were greatly for the interest of the poor, in this country at least, that the clergy should tread evenly in their own path of godly labour, without turning aside into the dubious walks of medicine. Their business is with that sacred oil which soothes the troubled waters of discord, and not with the aperient oils that stir up internal strife. They possess a balm for wounds of the soul and diseases of the inner man. They tend the jewel, and we the casket. Their labours are higher and holier than ours, but they do not include them.

For the "fiery Irish parson" of Stoke Gabriel, the attention and criticism he had earned for his efforts to treat Mrs. Lever did not cause him to rethink his opinions. He remained an adherent of Wallace's physianthropic theories. In 1890, the Rev. Nevill, described on the title page as a "sometime student of medicine at Trinity College Dublin, the Royal College of Surgeons and Meath Hospital, Dublin," published his own treatise, *The Biology of Daily Life*. (Cost: 3s 6d.) The premise:

ALL MEDICINES ARE DRUGS.

All drugging is detrimental in two ways. First, it puts foreign, and therefore disease producing material, into the texture of the body; and, by so doing, it also, secondly, strikes at the most fundamental law of organic life, viz., the law of continuous change. This law may be expressed thus: The existence of any organism depends upon its being able to maintain a process of change, in continuous adjustment with its surroundings. Drugs are essentially intractable and do not lend themselves to a process of change. In their mildest and least harmful forms, they obstruct and dam the river of the water of physical life. But this is at the best. **No language can convey an adequate notion of the miseries which drugs (whether introduced under the guise of food, drink, or medicine) have brought upon mankind.**

The alternative press found much to praise in the little volume. According to *The Theosophical Review*:

The conclusions he draws therefrom, if practically carried out, will lead in due course to a complete revolution of medical science, and an almost total disappearance of chemist's shops – nay even to that of the medical profession itself as it now stands constituted!

The Rev. John Henry Napper Nevill remained an active controversialist to the end of his days. He laboured in the vegetarian cause. He died in Stoke Gabriel in 1915. It should be noted that in June of 1888, at St. George's, Hanover Square in London, the vicar married Emma Burleigh Dawson, a widow with six children. Her first husband, of all things, had been a chemist! According to the book, *Devon's Amazing Men of God*, following word of the vicar's marriage, the unrequited doyenne of Sharpham Hall had that window walled over.

A Life of Open and Abominable Scandal

The Rev. Charles Rookes, Rector of Nymet Rowland

WE LIVE now in an era when, lamentably, scandals involving the moral failures of clergymen are not uncommon and will receive the full glare of media attention. It is then somehow important, if not exactly a comfort to the church itself, to understand that none of this is new. As far back as 1643 – an author by the name of John White released a furious book entitled *The First Century of Scandalous Ministers*. He accused the Church of England of tolerating "dumb dogs, ignorant drunkards, whoremongers and adulterers, sodomites, men unfit to live, crawling vermin, Popish dregs, priests of Baal, sons of Belial, unclean beasts," etc.

In the more than three and a half centuries that have passed since John White waxed so wrothful, it can be argued that perhaps no decade has seen a greater spate of bad clergydom in the Church of England than the 1840's. To name but a few: the Rev. Stephen Aldhouse of London who was transported to the Antipodes for seven years for bigamy; the Rev. Herbert Marsh (no less than the son of the Bishop of Peterborough), who died in a madhouse after he was exposed for having a child with a Parisian prostitute; and the Rev. Arthur Loftus of Fincham, who did Marsh one better – he hired two prostitutes to be his rectory servants, serving him in every way. [For more on Mr. Loftus, I invite the reader to see my *Blame it on the Norfolk Vicar,* also in this series.] The leader-writer of The Times of London threw up his hands in disgust:

> From the gravest enormities to the pettiest frauds, - from the highest crime to the lowest cunning, - from incest, adultery, cruelty, to avarice, chicanery, slander, we find the ministers of the church affording the worst and most flagrant instances of the vices we have named.

And that was in 1846! That was before the worst of the criminous clerics of the 1840's was to be found in one of the remotest villages in Devon. We speak of the Rev. Charles Rookes LL.B., the rector of Nymet Rowland, a man whose life was "an open and abominable scandal."

The details on Rookes' youth are quite sketchy. He was born in Devon about 1798. He entered Jesus College at Cambridge in 1817. He later acquired the title of "Doctor of Laws," apparently in Germany. He was ordained in 1827. His first church appointment came two years later when he was made rector of Teffont-Ewyas (or Evias), a Wiltshire village located in a "pleasant retired valley" nine miles from Salisbury. The same year, the Rev. Rookes was married to Mary Rudsdell, a daughter of the late Capt. Rudsdell of the Royal Navy. In 1837, the Rookes left Wiltshire and came to the Taw valley in Devon where the clergyman was now to be rector of the church of St. Bartholomew in Nymet Rowland.

It was a small village; the population at the time was not much more than 100. Nor is it all that much larger today. In 2006, *The Daily Telegraph*'s property section advised those seeking a West country home to give Nymet Rowland a visit, "it is a picturesque village in less well-trampled mid-Devon." There are several Nymet villages in Devon, strangely the smallest of which is called Broad Nymet. Etymologists argue over the ancient meaning of the word but the general consensus seems to be that a *nymet* was enclosed moorland, with perhaps some sacred connotation. As for the church of St. Bart's, it was one of Mr. Betjeman's favourites; he described it as rustic and remote with a "remarkable oak nave arcade."

The Rev. Charles Rookes served as rector of Nymet Rowland until his final disgrace and removal in 1849. However, from 1839, he chose to reside some eighteen miles away in Exeter. This move was made after his wife left him.

On 12 July 39, Mary Rookes sought "a separation from bed, board and mutual cohabitation, by reason of cruelty." Specifically, Mrs. Rookes charged that her husband had forced her to have a series of miscarriages. When she became pregnant, he demanded that she accompany him on long walks through the countryside. As a further precaution, he would press down on her stomach. He had insisted that this was for his wife's own good, barraging her with newspaper clippings detailing various cases where a woman had died in childbirth. Despite the graphic testimony, which "excited no small attention" in the county, the court found that Mary Rookes was "not entitled to the remedy she prayed for." Nonetheless, the Rookes remained apart, Mary choosing to reside in Bath.

The Rev. Rookes took up his solo residence in Hill's Court, off Long-brook Street, in the parish of St. Sidwell in Exeter. He lived there with a female servant, Mary Hanger. In 1841, Mary became ill with smallpox. To replace her, Mr. Rookes employed an Exeter girl by the name of Maria Brooks. She was one of three daughters of an impoverished widow living in Bear Street, then a narrow passage connecting South Street to the Cathedral close.

Mr. Rookes was now in his forties; Maria was just over twenty – perhaps 24, and, by accounts, a comely young lady. Her new employer certainly found her so as he took to giving her the occasional kiss by way of demonstrating his approval. Maria remained at Hill's Court for several months until her mother became ill and she had to go home to care for her. The rector was also concerned for the ailing Mrs. Brooks and visited their humble lodgings on several occasions. He made small contributions to their upkeep and one day he brought some linen to Maria and asked that she stitch him some new handkerchiefs. He requested that when she was finished with the little project, would Maria please bring the handkerchiefs to Hill's Court. Of course, she would. When she arrived with her handiwork, Mr. Rookes expressed his delight and said he would place them directly into the wardrobe in his bedroom. Would she come there with him? Of course, she would. One must know what then followed.

It was not long before Maria realized that she was pregnant. Mr. Rookes said that, for the sake of discretion, Maria must come back into his service immediately and live at Hill's Court where the matter might be quietly handled. He soon gave her a potion that, she later recalled, he described as being prepared from "something that will do you no harm, if it won't do you any good." She lost the baby.

By now, apparently, the manifold services of Maria Brooks had become indispensable to the Rev. Mr. Rookes. Old Mrs. Brooks, dodgy health or no, would have to do without her middle daughter. Maria would remain at Hill's Court as the rector's maid of all work and his lover. She was soon pregnant again. This development brought a visit to Hill's Court by Miss Eliza Brooks, the oldest of the Bear Street sisters. Eliza pitched in to Mr. Rookes. They had all felt that Maria would be safe in the employ of a clergyman and what instead had happened? The loss of the first baby had been a harrowing experience and Maria must not go through that again. By now, the Rev. Mr. Rookes was in tears, begging for the forgiveness of all the Brooks family. He said that the best would be made of a bad situation and Maria would be confined at Hill's Court and he would see to everything.

If naught else, the Rev. Rookes – on this occasion – proved to be a man of his word. A doctor was present for the birth of a boy in March of 1844. Mr. Rookes seemed to be a most delighted new father, attentive to mother and child and happy to hold his newborn son in his arms. The lad died on the third day. Now, it would fall to the clergyman to arrange for and finance a quiet burial for his son.

Meanwhile, Maria had also fallen quite ill. The local surgeon – a man apparently of great if questionable discretion - thought a specialist might be required. The obvious man to call was the renowned Exeter physician, Dr. Thomas Shapter. Rookes pleaded again with Maria and her sister that they not bring in Shapter for the great medico was a close associate of the all powerful Henry Phillpotts, Bishop of Exeter. Rookes could not risk the exposure and the speedy censure that would surely follow. Shapter was not called in. Fortunately, Maria rallied.

Maria Brooks remained at Hill's Court, in all, six years. There were four more pregnancies all ending in miscarriage. There was never any indication that these miscarriages had been forced as the rector's wife had previously claimed. Nonetheless, as a result of her series of misfortunes, Maria's health was not strong. Incredibly, old Mrs. Brooks then graciously agreed to allow her youngest daughter, Annie, to go reside at Hill's Court to assist her sister.

In 1847, the Brooks sisters took alarm at an increasing indication that the rector had transferred his affections elsewhere. At first, Maria dismissed the threat, claiming to have the clergyman's written promise to her. Her dismay can easily be imagined when she went to her workbox and discovered the document had been stolen. There were inevitable clashes at Hill's Court; Maria demanded to know the clergyman's intentions. The intruding woman, identified only as "Miss E," came under acrimonious discussion. It would all end badly, of course, as could have been predicted. The Brooks sisters removed themselves from Hill's Court. The repercussions for the clerical career of the Rev. Charles Rookes would not be long delayed.

The accuser who began the legal proceedings against Mr. Rookes was not Maria, but her mother. An aging and infirm widow, her sole support was the money to be earned by her three daughters. Now, one of those young ladies, Maria Brooks, had returned to her home in Bear Street broken in health and reputation. The case of *Brooks v Rookes* was called on 24 July 1849 in the Western Circuit at Exeter before Justice Sir Edward Vaughan Williams. The plaintiff was seeking compensation for the "seduction and loss of services" of her daughter, Maria.

The case to be brought against the Rev. Rookes was placed in the hands of Robert Collier QC, the "acknowledged leader of the Western Circuit." The star witness was Maria Brooks. The young woman testified that she had entered the rector's service at Hill's Court as a temporary replacement for the former housekeeper who had come down with smallpox. Maria said she stayed with him for about six weeks. During that time, she admitted that she had frequently allowed him to kiss her but she had excused the behaviour because it only happened when Mr. Rookes was "in drink." When her mother became sick, she left Hill's Court. Mr. Rookes showed the greatest concern for her mother. He called frequently, bringing food, brandy and offering "spiritual consolation." To help keep some income coming in, Mr. Rookes brought some cambric to Maria and asked that she make him some handkerchiefs. When she was done, he asked that she bring them to Hill's Court. She did as she was asked. At the rector's home, he asked to her to bring the sewing to his bedroom. When she entered the room, he quickly closed the door and then, for the first time, an intimacy took place between them.

After some weeks had passed, Maria reported that she was very likely with child. Mr. Rookes gave her something to drink, telling her the nostrum was not likely to harm her as it was "the very thing that married women take when they don't wish to bear children." She lost the baby in a fortnight.

Yet she remained in the service of the Rev. Mr. Rookes and, quite soon, was once again pregnant. This time, after some dispute, and at the insistence of her mother and sister, she was to have the child. At the rector's request, she was confined at Hill's Court and a nurse was provided for her needs. A doctor was summoned at the time of delivery and a baby boy was born in March of 1844 but lived only a few days. She thought that the Rev. Rookes had been truly fond of the infant and grieved at his quick passing. The rector handled the funeral arrangements.

She remained in the service of the Rev. Mr. Rookes until the middle part of 1848. She had become upset at the defendant's unhidden interest in a woman she had been instructed to identify only as "Miss E." Maria swore that the rector had talked to her frequently of marriage. When he had a wedding to perform in Nymet Rowland, he would often rehearse the marriage vows to her. There was, of course, the matter of his estranged wife still being alive. He promised that, immediately upon the death of Mary Rookes, they would be married. Maria also testified that he had written out his vow of marriage and she had kept it in her locked workbox. Apparently, the rector had found another key and stolen the paper, as she could not then produce it. A series of miscarriages having ruined her looks and her health, she had been cruelly discarded by her former lover and had to return to Bear Street as an insupportable additional burden to her widowed mother.

Eliza Brooks, Maria's older sister, described for the court the confrontation she had had with the Rev. Mr. Rookes at the time of her sister's second pregnancy. When she raised her voice to him, he told her to "Hush, hush, I'm a clergyman." Then, he began to cry. Eliza claimed that she told him, "Well you might cry for what you had done to Maria." Eliza stated that Rookes only agreed to co-operate after she had threatened to go to Thomas Latimer, the so-called "Cobbett of the West," the editor of *The Western Times*, an Exeter-based radical journalist and fierce opponent of Bishop Phillpotts. Latimer would be surely most interested in such a story to embarrass the Bishop in his own see. Mr. Rookes became angry and said she must absolutely not tell Latimer and he would do everything to handle Maria's confinement. When Maria was seriously ill, following the birth and tragic early death of the rector's child, Eliza had been told by Land, the local surgeon, to call in Dr. Shapter. Eliza said that Rookes flatly refused to send for that prominent physician; he became excited and said that if Shapter came, "the Bishop shall soon know all and I shall lose my gown." Fortunately, the ministrations of Dr. Land proved sufficient, assisted by the no doubt fervent prayers of the Rev. Rookes, and Maria pulled through.

Annie Brooks was the last of the sisters to take the stand. She said she had been at Hill's Court for almost two years, assisting her sister who was often weak and unwell following her pregnancies. Annie said that by early in 1848, the Rev. Mr. Rookes was frequently visited by "Miss E," who was sometimes accompanied by her sister, known only to the court as "Miss P." With or without Miss P, Miss E stayed quite late and quite alone in the rooms of Mr. Rookes. Maria became quite upset at this brazen demonstration that he would take a new favourite under her own eyes. There were frequent scenes. Both she and her sister were quite convinced that the Rev. Rookes had been intimate with Miss E.

Dr. William Land testified to having been present in Hill's Court in March of 1844 for the birth of a boy to Miss Maria Brooks. The infant was quite weak and survived only three days despite the best care, as requested by and paid for by the Rev. Mr. Rookes.

On several occasions, during the testimony of the witnesses for the other side, Rev. Rookes interrupted with vehement denials and tirades. Mr. John Greenwood, who had only that year taken silk as a Queen's Counsel, was defending Rookes and he was warned by Justice Williams that his client would be forcibly removed if necessary. Mr. Collier interpleaded, "Nay, let it go on, my Lord. I am convinced whatever he says will only more damage his case." Young Greenwood's task was certainly unenviable. Confronted with the salacious evidence provided by the sisters Brooks, Greenwood called no witnesses to challenge their version of events. His defense would be based on whether Mrs. Brooks could truly make any claim for compensation for the seduction of her daughter. What were her damages? Seduction cases were not infrequent and damages could be considerable, but only a few years prior to these events, Lord Chief Justice Tindal had cast his disfavour upon such actions, calling them "quasi-fiction." He decreed that proof of "loss of services" must be shown or the action must fail.

In this case, Greenwood stressed to the jury, Maria was not a minor – she was said to have been 24 when she was first hired by Mr. Rookes - and she was therefore free to make her own employment decisions and was no longer legally beholden to support her mother. She could hardly be "seduced" then from a home she was free to leave at any time. Maria also admitted that she was not a prisoner at Hill's Court. She had received a salary for her service, a portion of which she gave to her mother. The Brooks family had additionally received many gifts from the Rev. Rookes up until Maria left his service. As for the youngest, Annie, she also conceded that she went to join her sister with her mother's expressed consent.

As for Maria's story of having received a written promise to marry from the Rev. Mr. Rookes, Greenwood declared that a lie. The rector never made any such promise and her story of a stolen workbox was entirely spurious. Lawrence Stone, Britain's leading historian on divorce and domestic relations, writes that seduction suits were frequently brought to find a way to afford some "compensation to a seduced girl who did not have sufficient proof to launch a suit against her lover for breach of promise of marriage." Maria, the rector's counsel insisted, had no proof of any such breach.

Regardless, could anyone defend a married clergyman, albeit estranged from his wife for so many years, having such a relationship with a servant? Greenwood begged to remind the jury, however, that they were not part of an ecclesiastical tribunal. What they had before them was a civil case, not a criminal charge.

The rector of Nymet Rowland was not on trial. Whatever they might think about the conduct of the Rev. Mr. Rookes and this young woman, it must be remembered that she had quite plainly and willingly consented to remain with him for a period of six years. The only issue before the jury was – does old Mrs. Brooks deserve to be compensated for what the plaintiff had labeled "the seduction of her daughter." Why was this charge not brought as long ago as 1843? Instead, Greenwood reminded the jury, Mrs. Brooks - knowing the situation at Hill's Court - had allowed her youngest daughter, Annie, to also remain there for almost two years. This entire legal action, he charged, was more a persecution than a prosecution and a "base and iniquitous attempt at extortion."

On the second day, it was left to Justice Sir Edward Vaughan Williams to instruct the jury. Williams had some insight into the role and expectations of a clergyman. He was married to a clergyman's daughter. A fastidious man, the DNB described his courtroom demeanour as "laboured and somewhat embarrassed." Notwithstanding, he was respected for his judicial precision, "He probably gave occasion to fewer new trials on the ground of misdirection than any of his brethren." As he considered this case, Williams could only share with the jury their disgust with the conduct of a clergyman such as Mr. Rookes. However, it is not their role to award any damages out of a desire to punish Mr. Rookes. That is for his church superiors to care about. The only issue they must determine is what, if any, compensation is due to Mrs. Brooks for the "loss of services" of her daughter. As for the widowed plaintiff, Justice Williams reminded the jury that they must consider that Mrs. Brooks had, for a period of six years, allowed her two daughters to remain with Mr. Rookes at Hill's Court, "one in known and constant concubinage, the younger within the reach of seduction."

The jury of Exeter men went out only briefly before returning with a verdict for Mrs. Brooks. The jury thought the old woman should get the sum of £100 pounds for her troubles. A brief burst of applause and hoots of approval was angrily gaveled down from the bench. The local feeling was echoed across Britain as the Rookes case had drawn headlines as far away as Scotland: *Profligacy of a Clergyman of the Church of England.* In London, *The Times* loosed a thunderous denunciation from Fleet Street:

[The Rev. Rookes] led a life of open & abominable scandal, separated from his wife, carrying on adulterous intercourse with one woman, seducing a second, and living in open and promiscuous scandal with many others and who yet was permitted to continue his career of vice without any interference on the part of his ecclesiastical superiors … Our quarrel with the Bishop of Exeter is for having, with such means of investigation at his disposal, remained so long a time in ignorance of such a scandal; or, if he were aware of it, for having permitted it to remain so long unjudged and unpunished.

The Times was hardly alone in carrying this quarrel into the Episcopal Palace and placing it squarely on the desk of "Henry of Exeter" as his enemies had dubbed Bishop Phillpotts. This was a time of great theological ferment in the Church of England and Phillpotts was one of the great controversialists of the day. He was spending thousands of pounds annually in squabbles with clergymen over doctrinal niceties or what surplice they wore. Yet, the Bishop had managed to miss or, worse, he had ignored, a clergyman living a debauched existence within steps of the Cathedral. As the pressure mounted for action, it was obvious that the Rev. Rookes now had a much bigger foe than old Mrs. Brooks.

The Rev. Charles Rookes, LL.B., rector of Nymet Rowland was commanded to appear before the Bishop in the Chapter House of the Cathedral on 16 November 1849. The rector's new attorney, John Laidman, had already submitted a defense, citing the statute of limitations:

Every suit or proceeding against any Clerk in Holy Orders for offence against the laws Ecclesiastical, shall be commenced within two years after commission of the offence in respect of which the suit or proceeding shall be instituted, and not afterwards.

Rookes claimed that he had not been guilty of adultery, fornication or incontinence within two years from the date the Bishop had launched the proceedings against him. Several clergymen had used (and would continue to use) this tactic to wriggle their way out of punishment. While it was designed to protect innocent clergy from having to answer old allegations, with no living witnesses to defend them, the Archdeacon of York was among many to express concern:

Some limitation of time may in this case be expedient; but in many instances, the proofs of guilt do not come out for some time after the offence has been committed; and since all the old modes of proof are prohibited, the limitation to crimes committed within two years, seems to afford too great opportunities of escape to the guilty.

The proceedings were conducted by the Diocesan secretary, Ralph Barnes. The litany of sins laid at the feet of Mr. Rookes was again recited publicly. He had lived in a state of adultery with his housekeeper for six years. In March 1844, a doctor was fetched at two a.m. to assist at the birth of a child. The child died within days. All of the bills associated with that unhappy series of events had been paid for by Mr. Rookes. As for the claim that this misconduct was beyond the "statute of limitations," Barnes ruled it out brusquely. It was determined to be "wholly irrelevant." The Misses Brooks had testified to Mr. Rookes adultery with "Miss E," sinful conduct as recent as 1847. It was claimed that Miss E had repeatedly visited Hill's Court, remaining late and being entertained alone by Mr. Rookes. Given the clergyman's regrettable history – the investigators could come to only one reasonable conclusion as to the purpose of Miss E's visits. If these visits were innocent, why did not the rector present Miss E to be questioned on the matter? This adulterous liaison came well within the two-year time frame.

In sum, the case against the rector was quite damning. He had been convicted of "gross, frequent and hardened criminality." There was no other defense possible.

Mr. Rookes could not plead that he was tempted, and had fallen in an unguarded moment; neither could he plead youth for he was a man stricken in years.

The maximum punishment was pronounced: at the command of Bishop Henry Phillpotts, the Rev. Charles Rookes was to be deprived of his benefice at Nymet Rowland and "all its emoluments." Simply put, at last, "He is no longer fit to hold office as a clergyman."

The Rev. T.R. Dickinson was soon installed as the new rector of Nymet Rowland, a position he appeared to hold blamelessly for many years. As for the Rev. Mr. Rookes, he remained at Hill's Court, if not quietly. In 1851, he sued his solicitors claiming they had mishandled his case from the beginning, having promised him that he would "sail through" the courts undamaged. Mr. Rookes, acting as his own counsel, called as his lone witness, the Chancellor of the diocese, the Rev. George Martin. He demanded to know from the Chancellor if he thought the previous verdicts were against the evidence. To which, the reports stated, Martin answered "emphatically, no." The conduct displayed by Mr. Rookes in the courtroom was "unseemly throughout" and the jury "with haste" dismissed his lawsuit.

Despite his disgrace and deprivation, the Rev. Rookes remained in Exeter, a "clergyman without cure of souls." He occupied himself with his obsession to convert the Jews and even styled himself, in his frequent writings on the subject, as "the King of Kings." At his death in November 1867, he left a sizeable fortune of some £16,000. Of that, only fifty pounds would be left to his long abandoned but still surviving wife. The will was challenged but it could not be proven that Rookes was insane. The defenders of the will said the old clergyman had only a love of notoriety; he was not delusional. They cited one of his favourite expressions, "When I give 13 pence for a shilling, call me mad."

One of the last obituaries written of the Rev. Charles Rookes described him as "the most remarkable man in all Devonshire."

A Flagrant Miscarriage of Justice

The Rev. William Ewer Ryan, Vicar of Pilton

31 JULY 1891 was a summer Friday in Barnstaple. It was market day and the town's celebrated Pannier Market was typically crowded. Built off the High Street in the 1850's, the market replaced the earlier higgledy piggledy web of stalls and it could accommodate dozens of sellers purveying fresh vegetables and fruit and – on Friday's only – the separate Butcher's Row was also busy. The closeness of the butcher's offal to the produce vendors had troubled some more fastidious observers at first but the new building was wisely designed to be "very lofty & well ventilated" and a town historian soon described the Pannier market as "such as many a county town might well envy."

With so many people in the town for market day, it was always a convenient day for public meetings to be held. The Board of Guardians, for instance, met each Friday morning at 11:30 at the workhouse in Bear Street. The board administered the institution and was made up of a representative from all the local villages within the Barnstaple Union, including suburban Pilton, just across the river Yeo from the town. The Rev. William Ewer Ryan, the vicar of the Church of St. Mary in Pilton was there on the 31st of July to chair the board's midday session.

There was another meeting being held that day. This one was unscheduled. The Mayor of Barnstaple, Richard Lake, was in conversation with the local Police Superintendent George Songhurst. The subject was one of a most painful nature for both gentlemen. Supt. Songhurst had reported to the mayor that there was enough evidence now in police hands to accuse the aforementioned Rev. Ryan of having committed acts of "gross indecency" with several young men from North Devon.

Owing to the gravity of these charges and the prominent status of the accused clergyman, Mayor Lake determined that it would be best that he refer the matter to the board of magistrates. Whilst the mayor gathered his colleagues, he directed Songhurst to go to the vicarage in Pilton and deliver a summons to the Rev. Mr. Ryan to appear the very next day to answer the charges.

Saturday, 1 August, the mayor and five of his fellow magistrates, had gathered in the Guildhall (a handsome edifice, constructed in 1826). However, when the name of the Rev. William Ewer Ryan was called out in court, it went unanswered.

Residents of old Barum might not like to be reminded of the fact but there are those scholars of the days long gone past who will claim that Barnstaple was originally a suburb of Pilton, not the other way round as the matter has played out over the last millennium. Pilton's more defensible geographical location lost out to the more commercially advantageous site of Barnstaple. Over the passing centuries, there was even a time when the smaller village was reviled by the thriving cloth-makers of Barnstaple for competing against them with a shoddy product. Famously, in 1620, a Barnstaple man rose up to proclaim, "Woe, unto ye, Piltonians, who make cloth without wool!" We can now state that, happily, relations between the two communities have long since been pacified.

One of the points of evidence that Pilton was the more prominent of the early settlements was the presence of a priory, an offshoot of the Benedictine monks of Malmesbury Abbey. It was built in the time of King Athelstan in the 900's. St. Mary's Church stands now on the old Abbey site. Pilton church is well known amongst church-crawlers for the bizarre Jacobean hourglass affixed to the pulpit. C.G. Harper who traipsed the North Devon Coast in 1908 wrote:

> This fantastic object has acquired a very considerable celebrity in these days when every other tourist carries a photographic camera and hunts diligently for pictorial curiosities.

Harper was not pleased that the canny churchwardens were then brazenly demanding sixpence to take a snap. "Woe, unto ye, Piltonians!"

But, above all, literally, Pilton church is renowned for its bells. The Devonian church critic, John Stabb, declared them to be "with the exception of Exeter Cathedral, the finest peal of bells in the West of England." The campanologist W.H. Hamilton Rogers was moved to pen an ode to *The Great Bell of Pilton*:

> Sweet bell, how grand this peaceful Sabbath morn
> > Thy full note pulses through the sunlit air,
> As if from heaven's bright battlements 'twere borne,
> > From angel hands ringing the soul to prayer.

The Rev. William Ewer Ryan had been ringing the souls to prayer in Pilton since 1884.

Mr. Ryan first came to Pilton as curate to the longtime vicar in the village, the Rev. William Cradock Hall. Other than a brief hiatus, the Rev. Mr. Hall had been vicar of Pilton since 1837. Hall was born in Ireland in 1803. He and his wife had one son, Townshend Monckton Hall, who was born in 1845. Townshend was a delicate youth and was forced to leave Oxford before taking his degree. He returned to his father's vicarage, from which he found the strength to go forth to become one of the most respected amateur geologists of the period. His exploration of the "fossil-iferous Pilton bed" won him acclaim as "the leading authority on the geology of North Devon." He was honoured with an F.G.S., recognition as a Fellow of the Geological Society. In Barnstaple, he served in many capacities, including Vice-Chairman of the first school board. In Pilton, meanwhile, Townshend had developed a "devoted attachment" to his father's church, where, of course, he had spent most of his life. The younger Hall used some of his earnings to purchase the advowson of St. Mary's, becoming – in effect – his father's patron. He also superintended a refurbishment of the old church fabric, including a newly timbered roof.

In 1884, his father having passed into his eighties, Townshend determined that it was time to seek a curate who might assume some of the more demanding duties in the parish. He selected a distant Irish cousin of his, the Rev. William Ewer Ryan. The Ryans are one of the more flourishing clans in Ireland and the new curate was descended from the Ryans of Bally-mackeogh in County Tipperary. Educated and ordained at Trinity College, Dublin, the Rev. Ryan had held a series of Irish posts before he was invited by his cousin to cross the sea and come to St. Mary's Pilton. When he arrived in Devon, Mr. Ryan was 39, unmarried, and was accompanied by his widowed mother and his sister, Louisa Mary Ryan.

The following year, a most happy event would take place in Pilton as Townshend Monckton Hall and Louisa Mary Ryan were married at the parish church. Townshend then moved out of his father's vicarage to his newly built home at Orchard House, which he had constructed on land adjacent to the vicarage for himself and his young bride.

The Rev. Mr. Ryan, meanwhile, continued to assist the venerable vicar and soon was established as a popular figure in local church and civic society. He was described as an able speaker and preacher and, in the spirit of Townshend Hall, he too was more than willing to offer his services in various public capacities. When Rev. Hall died finally at the age of 85 in the winter of 1889, it was only natural that Townshend would recommend to the Bishop that the Pilton living be assigned to his brother-in-law. And, so it was done.

Tragically, only a few months later, on the 26th of May, Louisa Mary Ryan Hall died at the too young age of 37. Townshend, in his grief, retreated to Orchard House. He gave up most of his public duties and concentrated instead on plans for the addition of stained glass windows at St. Mary's to honour the memories of his father and his wife. He and the Rev. Ryan were working quite closely on these tributes. In fact, those plans were in progress at the time that Supt. Songhurst came to Pilton vicarage the afternoon of 31 July 1891 with a summons for the Rev. W.E. Ryan.

The following day, at noon, an unusual Saturday session for the Barnstaple magistrates was convened. The proceedings were held in the Guildhall, High Street. The building also housed the Barnstaple police: Mr. Songhurst commanding a doughty force of one inspector, a sergeant and nine constables. The large public hall, measuring 49 feet by 28 feet, was filled with locals drawn by the rapidly advancing word of the sensational charges pending against a local clergyman. Present to hear the case were the Mayor, Richard Lake, and several fellow magistrates including Col. Hugh Robert Hibbert of Broadgate House, a veteran of both the Crimea and the Indian mutiny; William Philip Hiern F.R.S., a local botanist and close friend of Townshend Hall; Samuel Goss, a chemist in the High Street, William Smyth, Esq., of Bear Street, and Charles Henry Basset of Pilton House in Pilton. The prosecutor was the Barnstaple Town Clerk, James Bosson. Everyone was present, it seemed, but the accused, the Rev. W.E. Ryan.

Supt. George Songhurst was called first by Mr. Bosson. The policeman affirmed that he had personally gone to the vicarage the previous afternoon at 3:15 to deliver the summons. He reported that he had placed the summons in the hands of the Rev. W.E. Ryan.

Though the Rev. Mr. Ryan had not deigned to appear to answer the summons against him, Mr. Bosson told the magistrates that it would be his "painful duty" nonetheless to present evidence which he believed would be quite sufficient for the magistrates to now issue a warrant for the vicar's arrest. Bosson indicated to the distinguished magistrates the presence in the Guildhall of seven young men. All of these, he said, were prepared to testify to having been subjected to "gross indecencies" at the hands of the Rev. Mr. Ryan. Rather than call them all, Bosson suggested that he would only need to introduce one of his witnesses at that time, choosing to save the remaining witnesses for the upcoming trial of the reverend gentleman. He declared that it was his wish to spare the magistrates the more disgusting details of the charges, a sentiment that was likely not shared by the ravenous public who had crowded the Guildhall that hot summer Saturday.

Mr. Bosson called 15-year old George Knill to the witness stand. George was described in the report on the case published in *The North Devon Journal* as "a bright lad." He was the youngest of seven children of Charles Knill, a Pilton stonemason. In the summer of 1891, George was employed as an errand boy for William Hunt & Son, ironmongers at 36 High Street in Barnstaple. On Wednesday, 8 July of that year, George was sent by his employers across the bridge to Pilton to retrieve the handle of a lawn mower from the vicarage. George said that when he arrived at St. Mary's, he met the Rev. Mr. Ryan. Together they went to the garden shed to locate the desired device. It was along the wooded garden path on the vicarage grounds that an assault "of a most revolting character" had occurred. The details were, of course, considered unfit for publication. *The North Devon Herald* dared only to report that the vicar "committed the indecent act himself and made the witness assist him." The implication is that the act involved masturbation on Mr. Ryan's part with the manual or oral assistance of "bright" young Knill. George testified that the 8th of July incident wasn't the first time something like this had happened; on a previous occasion, he was given a sixpence for his trouble and told by Mr. Ryan that nothing should ever be said to anyone about their relationship.

There was no one present to represent the interests of the Rev. Mr. Ryan and no questions were asked of George Knill by way of "cross-examination." After the lad had stepped down, Bosson again said that he would not trouble the magistrates further and would refrain from calling any of the other six boys who were present and ready to give similar evidence of a most outrageous character. The prosecutor said that the police had considered Mr. Ryan, more or less, under suspicion for as long as two years. Now, with this cadre of lads willing finally to testify against him, it was time to act against the vicar of Pilton.

The magistrates quickly agreed and granted the request for a warrant to be issued for the clergyman's arrest. Supt. Longhurst informed the magistrates that the Rev. Mr. Ryan's description had been sent by wire to all the likely ports of debarkation. Where had he gone?

The newspapers, county and beyond, were quickly drawn to the story of "The Serious Charge at Barnstaple." The ensuing "manhunt" was closely followed. It was very soon disclosed that the Rev. Ryan had written a letter of resignation addressed to the Bishop of Exeter, Edward Bickersteth. The letter was left at the Pilton vicarage for his patron, Townshend Hall. It was said that the clergyman had taken only a very small portmanteau with him when he left by trap for the railway station. At the time, there were three stations in Barnstaple: Town Station, where trains ran to the North Devon coast at Lynton; Barnstaple Junction, on the London and South West Railway, for trains to London and Exeter; and, lastly, the Great Western Railway station with trains connecting to the GWR main line at Taunton. It was at the last of these three stations that the Rev. Mr. Ryan was known to have purchased a ticket for the 5:50 train to Taunton. He left town, then, only some two and a half hours after the knock at the vicarage door from Supt. Songhurst. At the station, where he was recognized by a local acquaintance, Ryan said that he was going off to Athelney in Somerset where he had volunteered to do that Sunday's services as a favour to a fellow clergyman.

There was no trace of the Rev. Mr. Ryan beyond Taunton; he most certainly, and to no one's great surprise, did not appear in the pulpit that Sunday in Athelney. From Taunton, he could have gone anywhere by rail. He could have taken a Great Western train south to Exeter (the line's route to the Southwest was much longer than that of their rivals at the London & SW Railway and the GWR was ridiculed as "The Great Way Round.") In Mr. Ryan's case, it was much more likely that he took the train north to Bristol's Temple Meads station. From there, he could go east to lose himself in London or head for the Channel ports. The prevailing theory in North Devon, however, was that he likely caught a train from Bristol to the west into Wales. His goal would be to reach a port, such a Milford Haven, where he might catch that evening's mail-boat to his native Ireland.

While all this might be a fascinating subject for devotees of the railway and ferry timetables, back in Barnstaple, the anger was building. According to *The Exeter Flying Post*, "Rumours of Ryan's habits have been rife in the town for a year or two past." Yet, nothing had been done and now the accused man had been clumsily allowed to absquatulate. "There is a strong feeling in the town that [Rev. Mr. Ryan] should have been apprehended on a warrant, as the summons gave him the opportunity of evading justice."

The Western Daily Mercury placed the blame on Mayor Lake. He had been fully apprised by Songhurst of the charges that were to be brought against the clergyman and the willingness of the various young men to testify. Surely, there was enough information in hand to order Mr. Ryan's arrest yet the mayor was too timid to authorize a warrant to take such a prominent individual into immediate custody without some support from other magistrates. *The Mercury* suggested that perhaps the mayor had gotten the exact result that he wished for, i.e. permitting the disgraced vicar to escape and thereby avoid a scandalous public trial that would have been a terrible ordeal for the church and for Rev. Ryan's prominent and respected patron, Townshend Hall. *The Mercury* was indignant:

> The old feeling is rife that there is one interpretation of the law
> for the rich and another for the poor … It is never possible to
> cloak a scandal of this kind, and it is a pity that anything should
> be allowed to occur to give it undue prominence in the public
> eye or to bring the administration of justice under the slightest
> shade of suspicion in connection with it.

Nor was the criticism of the North Devon authorities limited to the county press. From London, a blast came from the pen of the irrepressible Henry Labouchere MP editor of the muck-raking weekly *Truth*:

> Not even the most ordinary precautions were taken to serve the
> ends of justice. If Mr. Ryan had been a workingman, he would
> have been arrested under a warrant … It is a flagrant miscar-
> riage of justice.

As the perfunctory search continued into mid-August without any likely success, Labouchere persisted in his abuse of the Barnstaple police – a force he described as "tardy and stupid." He informed his readers that, "It is asserted very plainly that there was a general desire to let Mr. Ryan escape." Respectable friends had sounded the alarm and the clergyman had fled and was now beyond the reach of justice and punishment for his abominable crimes.

For Labouchere, this was a subject of the greatest personal interest. In 1885, as the radical MP for Northampton, he had authored the Criminal Law Amendment that first criminalized private acts of homosexual conduct. Any male person convicted of "gross indecency" with another male person was guilty of a misdemeanour and liable to a sentence of a maximum of two years, with or without hard labour. It is essential to point out that the Rev. William Ewer Ryan's bolt to escape prosecution for his crimes of "gross indecency" came against the very recent backdrop of the sensational "West End Scandals" in London. That had been the first major test of the new law. Then, as in the case of the Rev. Mr. Ryan, a prominent suspect was alerted by his influential friends and permitted with a wink and a nod to flee to the continent to avoid arrest for similar offences. Lord Arthur "Podge" Somerset, an unmarried son of the Duke of Beaufort and an equerry to the Prince of Wales, had been named to the police as one of the society gentleman who patronized a male brothel on Cleveland Street. A warrant had been issued for his arrest but Lord Arthur made good his escape the night before. A few "Post Office telegraph boys" were left to take the fall. Labouchere then charged in the House of Commons that there had been a cover-up at the highest levels; Lord Arthur had been warned by Gen. Dighton Probyn to "make himself scarce" on direct instructions from the Prime Minister, Lord Salisbury. When the government bench issued a denial on behalf of the Marquis, Labouchere created an uproar in the Commons by declaring, "I do not believe Lord Salisbury." While Labouchere was temporarily suspended from the House, the public outrage forced the Prime Minister to eventually make a statement in the House of Lords. Salisbury insisted that he had conveyed no secrets as he had no secrets to convey. The P.M. admitted that he had, in fact, spoken with Gen. Probyn the evening of Lord Arthur's departure but recalled the conversation only as a "brief and casual interview to which he did not attach the least importance." Lord Salisbury sat down to great cheers.

Lord Arthur would spend the rest of his life in Italy. Where, we might well ask, had the Rev. W.E. Ryan gone to ground? If, as suspected, he had gone back to Ireland, it would not have been wise. The news of his disgrace had surely reached Tipperary and had he been spotted, the public clamor that followed his escape would have forced the police to act. It was more likely that Ryan would have followed the more well trodden path laid out by Lord Arthur and others to the continent. There was also the possibility of Australia where Rev. Ryan did have a brother, a physician, who had emigrated thither. Australia was still red on the map but it was likely far enough away that the cost of arrest and transportation home for a trial would have made any such eventuality prohibitively expensive. Lastly, of course, there was the option later suggested by King George V who opined, "I thought such men shot themselves." There is no record that Ryan took that way out.

Was he guilty? Given the promptitude of his flight, it would seem more than merely probable. It also appears clear that he was given the chance to escape not out of any respect or consideration for himself but more for the feelings of Townshend Monckton Hall. A respected local resident, nationally honoured for his scientific accomplishments, patron of Pilton church, member of the school board, Hall was also a man still grieving over the recent deaths in succession of his father and his wife. Now, added to his pain, his brother-in-law, a man he had personally summoned to Pilton, had been publicly charged with crimes of a revolting character. It was probably felt sufficient that Ryan be given the ultimatum to leave or face arrest, trial and conviction for his misconduct. Just leave now. He "made himself scarce."

A few months later, the announcement was quietly made that the Rev. William Bagley would be the new vicar of Pilton, the position having been "rendered vacant by the resignation of the Rev. W.E. Ryan." The weekly, *The Reynolds Newspaper* found some grist for its consistently anti-clerical views:

> The reverend State parson (i.e. Mr. Ryan) was "held in high esteem in the district." There is the danger. In spite of repeated warnings, parents continue to believe in the honour of parsons. It is not surprising, consequently, that they are so frequently shockingly undeceived.

As for Townshend Monckton Hall, he remained at Orchard House, near his father's old vicarage in Pilton. He lived only a short while longer, dying in 1899 at the age of 54. In an obituary published in one of the many scientific journals that noted his passing, no mention was made of the Ryan scandal. However, the author did state that Hall's final years were marked with sadness, "Mr. Hall, who had always led a somewhat solitary life, became naturally more secluded than beforetime."

An Odious Accusation

The Rev R.L.P. Samborne,
Rector of Ashreigney

The season has now come to an end; men and women jaded in the pursuit of those artificial pleasures which, as a late statesmen said, rob life of its enjoyment, will soon separate to seek a fresh and more healthful excitement by sea and shore, by loch and river, on mountain and moor, now, while the summer is at the height of its pomp and beauty, and onward till the genial glow of autumn yields to the stormy presage of the year's decay.

SO WROTE *The Times* on the 3rd of August 1878 in their annual leader on the end of another London season. The exodus from Town was about to begin. Londoners by the thousands were fleeing a summer that, even for the capital city, had been peculiarly capricious, "Tropical one day and arctic the next, and alternating week by week between the most exasperating extremes."

Among those making ready to levant London for the countryside was the Bayswater family of Andrew Prescott. Mr. Prescott was a principle in the City banking house of Prescott, Cave, Buxton & Loder, a firm doing business at 62 Threadneedle Street, within steps of the great Bank itself.

Prescott, who claimed lineal descent from Oliver Cromwell, was a married man; his wife Emma and he had three very young children. This year, the Prescotts were going to be staying in the remote Devon village of Ashreigney. For Prescott *pere*, the draw was the shooting. Ashreigney is located on the vast hunting preserve of the Earl of Portsmouth, Master of Foxhounds. From his seat at nearby Eggesford, Lord Portsmouth's demesne covered some 400 square miles. The opportunities for game and sport were highly regarded. A sportsman named Brooksby, writing in his *Hunting Counties of England, a Guide to Hunting Men*, thought it all quite jolly:

> The stag will no doubt be the primary object of a journey of five or six hours from London, for none but the most ardent seeker of change will be likely to travel so far merely to extend his experience of foxhunting. Yet, being on the spot, here is the opportunity of seeing the latter sport right well enacted according to the requirements of the west.

While Prescott would be out stalking stags or hounding foxes, his wife and bairns could enjoy the fresh air and beautiful Devon countryside, escaping the heat, smell, noise and general dullness of post-season London.

In June, Prescott had spotted an ad in *The Field* sporting magazine, about a three-month lease from August to October being offered on the rectory in Ashreigney. Certainly, that sounded ideal for a family. Prescott had opened negotiations with the Rev. Richard Lane Palmer Samborne, rector of St. James, Ashreigney.

In 1878, the year our story begins, the Rev. Mr. Samborne was fifty. He was born near Plymouth, educated at Rugby and Balliol College, Oxford. Ordained in 1854, he had been the rector of Ashreigney since 1855. The name of the village is a curious one with multiple theories as to its origin. Chips Barber, in his *Place Names of Devon*, suggests that the locals knew it at Ring's Ash but the gentry thought Ashreigney was a more proper sounding name for a village and – as usual, isn't it – the gentry won in the end. The gentry's effete wishes notwithstanding, and for some reason lost in history, the villagers of Ashreigney were known as "dog-eaters." Nonetheless, there was a pretty North Devon church, dedicated to St. James. The Sambornes lived at the partly thatch-roofed rectory, some half-mile to the north of the church. It was said to be "a good residence with 78 acres of glebe." The rector resided there with his wife, Emma, born in County Down, Ireland and their four children, two daughters followed by two sons. The commodious rectory housed as many as seven servants. An earlier rector had described the village situation as "high and healthy.

It all seemed perfect for Prescott's needs and the terms being offered were £150 for the three months, half to be paid in advance. This seemed quite agreeable to the fiscally astute banker, however, as is probably still a wise practice today, Mr. Prescott said he would make no commitments until his wife could get a few more details on the property. The Rev. Mr. Samborne understood completely and said that his wife would be glad to provide whatever information might be needed to determine the rectory's suitability for the Prescott establishment. Mrs. Prescott promptly wrote to Ashreigney with her list of questions, most of which would not be out of line coming from a modern holiday-maker: the number of bedrooms, linen facilities, staffing questions (well, maybe not so much today). Overriding these logistical details, however, were the Prescott's concerns about the health of the village. Nor were such questions unusual or at all out of line. It is unlikely the Prescotts regularly read *The Sanitary Record*, however, in an article in that July's issue, Dr. Frank Buckland referenced

> The case of a little town in Devonshire, situated on a brook polluted with every description of filth, on which the population is entirely dependent for water. My enquiry whether fever was not prevalent elicited the reply, "We are never without it."

Devon bound holiday-makers were advised to ask questions first: "An honest declaration of the freedom from infectious disease of the chief places of interest is of great importance."

Mrs. Prescott, therefore, specifically asked about the quality of the drinking water at the rectory and – in general – the health of the village population. Mrs. Samborne sent a letter in reply to London addressing the issues raised, point-by-point. As for the health concerns, the rector's wife boasted "We have very good water" and there is no disease in the village beyond the ordinary. The rector added his assurances,

> I can simply tell you, as an instance of the healthiness of the house and place, that we have had no illness (except colds and such ailments, which necessarily visit humanity) for the 23 years we have been here, and the doctors have been paid very little by me.

Mrs. Prescott was delighted to have that intelligence and signaled her acceptance; Mr. Prescott then agreed to the terms and the lease was signed in late July. The first payment of £75 was made. The Sambornes vacated the rectory. Mrs. Samborne and the children, going against the traffic, so to speak, left for temporary lodgings in London. The rector remained an extra day, staying in the village, to ensure that the Prescotts got settled in. He then followed his family to London. The Prescott family had arrived in Ashreigney on the 3rd of August, the very day of *The Times* leader; just another family seeking "fresh and more healthful excitement."

Within a day or two after the Prescotts arrived in Ashreigney, having transported their bag and baggage from Bayswater, they discovered scarlet fever had struck in the village. They also determined that the rectory's water supply was vile and undrinkable. The furious Prescott gathered his family and removed them from Ashreigney immediately. He took himself directly back to London to confront the Rev. Mr. Samborne. When he arrived at the Samborne's lodgings, the rector's son informed him that his father would be unable to see him because, at the moment, the clergyman was in mourning. Mrs. Ellen Samborne had died that very day. She was 48. The cause of death was scarlet fever.

It was 15-year old Walter Samborne who had the unpleasant task of sending the irate Prescott away. The banker said he would take his leave out of respect for their grief but he told the youth that the Prescott family would not stay at Ashreigney rectory one night and he was prepared to insist upon a full refund. He expected to hear from the Rev. Samborne on the matter as soon as possible. When Prescott did hear from Rev. Samborne, he was not pleased. The rector insisted that the outbreak of fever in the village was not anything that could have been predicted. The water at the rectory was perfectly safe. Mr. Prescott had leased the property for three months and the rector was expecting full payment of £150 that October. Both sides hardened their positions on the matter and on 16 June 1879, before Lord Justice Denman in Common Pleas Court, London, the case of Prescott v. Samborne was called before a special jury. Andrew Prescott was demanding a refund of the £75 paid in advance and all expenses incurred in the going and coming from Ashreigney the previous August. Rev. Samborne had counter-claimed, demanding the entire £150 as has been agreed, plus costs for "the use of a cob, a harness and trap, the wages of a gardener and boy, shooting etc."

Prescott was charging that the Rev. Mr. Samborne and his late wife had made "fraudulent misrepresentations" as to the healthiness of the rectory and village. The Prescotts had arrived to find "a very dangerous place" and had therefore withdrawn. Their counsel WC Harrison QC told the court that both Mr. and Mrs. Prescott had made diligent inquiries prior to taking the lease. With their young children in mind, they had placed a particular emphasis on the health of the village. In return, they had been completely assured by the Sambornes that the water was good and that there was no sickness in the village. What did they find on their arrival? The water at the rectory was not potable, being "impregnated with drainage." And, tragically, there was an "epidemic of scarlet fever" in the district. Among the victims, most painfully for all concerned, was the defendant's wife. Obviously, the plaintiff's counsel argued, the Prescotts had not been told the truth by the Sambornes and should therefore be refunded their initial payment and recompensed for their travel and other incidentals incurred in the long journey to and from Devon.

John Charles Day was the QC for the rector of Ashreigney. He said he would address the two major points raised by Mr. Prescott. Firstly, the water. The late Mrs. Samborne had written to Mrs. Prescott that "We have very good water," and indeed, Day told the court, that was and remained the truth. The rectory draws water from three sources, including a well of the "purest spring water," ample for all the drinking needs of the Prescotts, a family no larger than the Sambornes. That well had since been tested and the water had once again been found to be quite healthy. There was also a second well with water that was restricted to household uses, and, finally, a cistern that collected rainwater. All of this had been detailed to the Prescotts during the exchange of correspondence prior to the lease being signed. Moreover, the rectory servants - who were, of course, accustomed to these riparian arrangements - had all been retained by the Prescotts. In sum, the drinking water at Ashreigney rectory was perfectly safe.

The more difficult matter, Mr. Day continued, and the one that had touched the Samborne family so tragically, was the question of disease. There was no way the Sambornes could have known that scarlet fever would strike in their village. At the time the Prescotts made their commitment to come to Ashreigney, there were no cases in their area. On 10 August 1878, "The Public Health Report" had declared that scarlet fever was "prevalent in Sheffield and Birmingham." Some cases of "mild" scarletina had been reported in Devon but not in any locations near to Ashreigney. Scarlet fever, or scarletina, was a frightening disease; it struck unpredictably, it was virulently contagious and often deadly. The contemporary medical texts warned that exposure to the patient and anything he or she had touched was dangerous. The virus' "tenacious attachment" to objects made it extremely portable, often striking hundreds of miles from the initial case. Symptoms came on abruptly. In mortal cases, the sufferer's skin "could be likened to the appearance of a boiled lobster." In the last stages, the patient slipped into a "more or less stupor, with transient delirium and sudden starting or twitching of the extremities." It was no disease to take lightly. It had come to Ashreiegney without warning.

The local doctor testified that a resident had gotten the fever on the last day of July. The cottage where the patient resided was some 600 yards from the rectory. The local doctor insisted that this case was not known to anyone in Ashreigney until after the rector and his family had left. It was, more than likely, however, the source of the infection that felled Mrs. Samborne, who did not become ill until after her arrival in London. The village case was not a particularly serious one and the patient survived; unfortunately, the rector's wife had also suffered from a weak heart and that had undoubtedly made her case a mortal one.

Justice Denman suggested from the bench that this was a case that, given the tragic loss of Mrs. Samborne, that both parties would well consider settling. Mr. Day, however, said it was "quite impossible." His client, the Rev. Mr. Samborne would never consider "buying off a charge of fraud against his dead wife." Mr. Prescott had made an "odious accusation" against his beloved wife. Worse, he had first cruelly made that insulting charge when her grieving husband had not even had the time to bury her. Mr. Prescott, a London banker of mature age, had angrily confronted Walter Samborne, a boy of 15, whose mother had only just died of a horrible disease. The Sambornes had no intention of settling.

Lord Denman instructed the jury at great length. Their duty, he said, was to decide whether the Samborne's assurances to the Prescotts had been their true beliefs at the time of the lease being signed or whether the rector and his late wife were guilty of dishonesty or suppression of facts. His Lordship acknowledged that it was an unusually painful case as Mrs. Samborne was not present to defend herself. Indeed, it might be fairly stated that it was the circumstances that led to her death that prompted the entire matter. The jury decided "at once" – *The North Devon Herald* reported that it took "only a minute" - that there was no fraud on the part of the Sambornes. Still, in a solomonic judgment, the jury decreed that the rector would not get the outstanding £75 from Mr. Prescott.

The Rev. Mr. Samborne and his family remained at the rectory in Ashreigney until his death in November of 1887. The cause of death was not reported.

Notorious Over All of Exeter

The Rev. Arthur Whipham, Rector of Gidleigh

"If there be any man to whose happiness marriage is more necessary than to that of another, it is a country clergyman." Anthony Trollope, The Bertrams

AS WITH most things, if not all things, Trollope here was spot on point. Consigned to an isolated vicarage, perhaps a day's ride from "gentle-manly" companionship, a clergyman's happiness and even sanity were dependent upon the strength he drew from his own hearth. Surrounded by a loving wife and a cheerful brood, the lonely labours of rustic parish life were bearable. More though than simply seeing that the stew was hot, little Nigel's fever was coming down and the flues were kept clean, the clergyman's wife was most importantly a helpmate and confidante. She would also be expected to share the load of daily duties in the church. The Rev. Francis Pigou, the Dean of Chichester, who wrote a series of tracts for clerical families, advised young women pondering a clerical marriage to fully understand, "When you marry a clergyman, you marry his work." Again, that work went beyond sitting with the dying wife of the local miller or arranging the flowers for a holy day, a clergyman's wife was expected to set an example in her own marriage, of devotion, submission, and fidelity. Anything less could ruin her husband's career. This, however, is the story of the Rev. and Mrs. Arthur Whipham of Gidleigh.

As anyone who has had the good fortune (and, alas, the required fortune) to stay at the Gidleigh Park Hotel near Chagford in Devon, the drive to the inn through the magnificent scenery is truly an unforgettable one. On the very edge of Dartmoor, Gidleigh has long been one of the most inaccessible but celebrated beauty spots in the realm. In *Murray's Handbook for Travelers in Devon & Cornwall*, from the 1850's, intrepid would-be visitors were told the journey was well worth the then strenuous effort:

> Gidleigh Park is well known as a magnificent scene of wood and rock, where the Teign hurries down a declivity, and, in the course of ages, has wormed a deep channel in the granite, which it traverses with a roar that may be heard at a great distance.

White's Devonshire Directory of 1850 acknowledged that the vast acreage of Gidleigh Park was "fruitful only in rabbits." But the beauty of it all was singular:

> A steep descent from the park to the river Teign is studded by enormous rocky protuberances … The roaring stream at the bottom of this descent, the wooded front of the bold bank that rises on the opposite side, and the vast masses of rock on either hand, gray with moss, or dark with ivy, render this part of the park truly romantic.

The river rushes and splashes through the village, passing the small Holy Trinity church. A half-mile away stood Gidleigh Park house. The Whipham family had owned the park property for less than fifty years, purchasing it from a Bartholomew Gidleigh. The original Park House was built in the 1500's by the Prouz family. In 1835, fresh from Trinity College, Oxford, the Rev. Arthur Peregrine Whipham arrived to be the new rector at Holy Trinity. He took up residence at Gidleigh Park house. He was, at the time of his arrival, unmarried. He firstly sunk his energies and some considerable money into a restoration of the church that was completed in 1841. It was time then to find a wife.

In fact, it wasn't until 1843 that the rector brought his bride to Gidleigh Park. That August, he had married Frances Stephens Huxham, one of the twin daughters of a solicitor from Bishopsteignton. The Rev. Mr. Whipman was now 32; his new wife was considerably younger, nearing her 18th birthday. Arthur and Frances settled in at Gidleigh and began a family. By the 1851 census, they had five sons. Another son and a first daughter followed in the new decade. In all, the Whiphams had eight children, a second daughter died at birth. Despite the fecundity of the marriage, it was a decidedly unhappy one with "frequent differences" between them.

They separated for the first time in 1858. Rev. Mr. Whipham had heard disquieting reports about his wife's relationship with a physician in Moretonhampstead. There were arguments in which Frances counter-charged that Arthur had behaved improperly with one of "the common servant girls" at Gidleigh Park. The rector agreed to allow Frances and their daughter a guinea a week if she would leave Gidleigh (and any of her favourite Devonshire doctors) and go to live with her parents who were then residing on the continent. Frances found employment as a tutor, claiming among her students a son of the Archbishop of Canterbury. However, the promised weekly guineas from Gidleigh stopped coming and the Huxhams were apparently not willing to support their daughter and grandchild and ordered her to go back to Devon and seek out her husband.

As for the rector of Gidleigh, "misfortune had befallen him," as his legal counsel would later tell the courts. Arthur had signed a bond for one of his brothers and, after the bond was defaulted, Arthur found himself in jail for several months in 1859. His financial affairs had become decidedly muddled; he had been forced to let Gidleigh Park and was now occupying a cottage on Holy Street, the lane that connects the village with Chagford. It was there that husband and wife (with their daughter Laura in tow) were reunited. It did not go well. Arthur said not a word and took his leave. His old servant, Elizabeth Bourn, was left to care for his wife and childthem.

Frances found the cottage completely unsuitable. There were no locks on any of the doors. In some of the rooms, a person would be forced to walk on the joists as the floorboards were missing. She remained there for three weeks before leaving for Exeter. There, she took rooms with a Mrs. Sparshatt, who had a lodging house at 33 Southernhay in the parish of St. Sidwell. The area was described as the "finest residential section" of the cathedral city. Mrs. Sparshatt – as with all successful landladies – expected to be paid for her rooms. In June of 1861, she sued the Rev. Arthur Whipham for £47, the cost of his wife's room and board for the previous six months.

Mr. Flood, who represented the wife of the rector of Gidleigh told Judge John Tyrrell that this was a most lamentable action. The Whiphams "don't appear to have lived a very happy life." He recounted the terms of their original separation and the events leading up to her return in October of the previous year. She came home to a husband who would not even stay under the same roof with her. She was left in an uninhabitable cottage, with doors that would not secure, on the very edge of the wilds of Dartmoor, with no more protection than an elderly female servant. Her husband had left her and their daughter without food and without a single farthing to get any. Mrs. Whipham had remained in the cottage for almost three weeks. She had written a letter to her husband expostulating with him for his "cruel and unmanly conduct." When he did not even reply to that appeal – which had been made more in the interests of her child – Mrs. Whipham was forced to seek lodgings more suitable.

After Frances Whipham testified to these facts, she was questioned by Merlin Fryer, the solicitor for the Rev. Mr. Whipham. He reminded her of the reports that linked her to a "medical gentleman residing in Moretonhampstead." Frances said the story was untrue, it was nothing but "rumours spread by wicked men." She insisted that she had never gotten down on her knees to beg her husband's forgiveness for any "improper conduct." She did admit that she was aware that her husband had been briefly imprisoned for debts resulting from the defaulted note he had signed for his brother.

Betty Gower, Mrs. Whipham's servant, told the court that when they arrived at the cottage in Chagford, the rector's little girl asked her father for some meat. He gruffly told the child, "I have no meat for myself and none for you." The servant said that none of the shops in Chagford would let them have any food "on trust," apparently on the rector's orders.

Mrs. Sparshatt then came forward clutching her outstanding bill for accommodating Mrs. Whipham and her hungry child. That closed the case for the prosecution.

Mr. Fryer said that the Rev. Mr. Whipham had no legal responsibility to put his wife up in such a costly establishment as that run by Mrs. Sparshatt. His wife had left the Holy Street cottage without any reason or cause whatsoever. It was true that he did not want her in his home and he would not stay there with her owing to the ill-feelings between them. The law does not compel a husband to reside with his wife. It was a fine labourer's cottage and the conditions had been good enough for the rector and they should have been good enough for his wife. After his "misfortunes", he did not have the money to improve the house to suit the tastes of Mrs. Whipham. He had instructed his servant that his wife and child should be provided with all their necessities. Despite that assurance, Mrs. Whipham had left without good and sufficient reason to take expensive lodgings that she certainly knew her husband could not afford.

The rector of Gidleigh took the stand to say that he had formerly been a man of some means but an unfortunate speculation and the legal problems of a defaulted bond had reduced him now to living off his clerical income. The poor parish of Gidleigh afforded him only £100 a year. From that, he was educating his sons, who were attending a school "for the sons of gentlemen and the clergy" in Sussex. He was fully prepared to escort his wife back to the cottage in Chagford that very day. He just could not stay there with her.

> Judge Tyrell: Is it becoming of a clergyman and a gentleman to leave his wife and child alone in an unsecured house with only an elderly female servant?
>
> Mr. Whipham: I had no choice.
>
> Judge Tyrell: And be murdered, I suppose.
>
> Mr. Fryer (for Rev. Whipham): We do not very often hear of such cases as those now.
>
> Mr. Flood (for Mrs. Whipham): They used to be common enough a few years ago.

The only other witness for the rector was his servant, Elizabeth Bourn. She testified that her instructions were to make sure that Mrs. Whipham and her child were comfortable and had the food they needed. The observer from *Trewman's Flying Post* thought the old woman gave her evidence in a "hesitating, not to say prevaricating manner."

Given the tone of his earlier question, Judge Tyrell's ruling came likely as no surprise. He thought that the rector's decision to abandon his wife and child in such a cottage, without provision or protection, fully justified Mrs. Whipham's decision to find lodgings elsewhere. Whether she could have found a place more affordable than Mrs. Sparshatt's was not the question. The bill that the landlady had submitted was fair and the rector would have to pay it.

Following the Sparshatt matter, the Whiphams made another bid to live harmoniously under the same roof but it was just not to be. Mrs. Whipham again moved out, and the rector agreed to let her two rooms at Berrydown, an "ancient stone farmhouse" on Dartmoor, owned by a local farmer, John Rowe. Though separated again, the rector would not be free of his wife's bills. By July of 1862, he was back in court, being sued by Messrs. Pearse, drapers on Fore-Hill Street in Exeter, who had sold to Mrs. Whipham, a variety of goods in the amount of £16.

This time, he won. Mr. Whipham said he had gone to Exeter and personally walked the streets and visited every tradesman, instructing them that his wife does not enjoy his credit. As for their latest separation, he said it had been prompted by his wife's conduct; in fact, her language was "so shocking" that he had to demand that she leave "for the sake of the morals of our children." His solicitor, once again Mr. Fryer, put the questions to Mrs. Whipham:

> Q: Have you not called your husband, in the presence of your children and of his servants, a brute, a beast and a blackguard.
> A: Very likely, for he deserves them all. He has treated me like a brute in every way.
> Q: Didn't you once say, also in the presence of your children, that Mr Whipham would take advantage of any and every woman in his house?
> A: Yes, I have grounds for saying so.
> Q: You say so in a public court?
> A: Yes.
> Q: Did you not also say, in the presence of your children, that Mr. Whipham had some bad disorder and that he caught it of some woman in the village?
> A: I am not in a position to say what I might have said when excited.
> Q: Did you not also say that you should be allowed to marry the man you loved?
> A: I daresay I did. Of course, if he were dead, I should be able to do as I like about that.

The rector, of course, denied any such connection with the unnamed "woman in the village" or any "bad disorder" of the sort suggested.

This time, Mrs. Whipham would find Judge Tyrrell much less supportive. She had insisted that her purchases at the Pearses were for her essential clothing needs. "What does a woman living in a farmhouse," the judge inquired, "need with silk scarves and pearl buttons?" When she suggested that the rector had "robbed" her of her own dresses, the judge would not let it pass. "Robbed you? You don't seem to know that all those things belong to your husband." In the end, Tyrrell sent the Messrs. Pearse away unpaid: "They should have known that what was notorious over all of Exeter."

The antics of the Whiphams were mocked in the press. *Trewman's Flying Post* had headlined their report on the case, *Scenes of Clerical Life*, a wry reference to the new stories from George Eliot. However, the notoriety of the miserable Whiphams was far from over. As already established, Mrs. Whipham and her daughter had recently been living at Berrydown, near the stone circle at Scorhill on the moor. The owner, John Rowe, was a prosperous farmer, employing a dozen or so lads to till his 170 acres. Now in his late sixties, John and his wife Agnes had raised five sons of their own. Their second son was Philip. He lived with his parents at Berrydown. Philip was 26.

In August of 1862, the Whiphams were again consigned to living under one roof, at the rectory in Gidleigh. Not surprisingly, they occupied separate bedrooms. On the night of Sunday, the 31st, the Rev. Whipham went to stay at an inn in Chagford. On this occasion, however, he left "watchers" behind. They settled in on what was a wet night. Philip Rowe's arrival from Berrydown, only a few hundred meters to the south of the village, did not pass unnoticed. Simply to pay a nocturnal visit to the wife of a clergyman living unhappily with her husband might not have been the done thing but it was hardly damning. More evidence would be needed for any divorce proceeding. The "watchers" were patient. When the illicit lovers retreated to Mrs. Whipham's bedroom, the time was then right to move. At some appointed signal, action was taken. To quote the press reports of the ensuing divorce case, "the local police constable surprised the paramours in bed together." That might have been a bit of overkill as adultery was not a crime punishable in a police court. However, surely the local plod would (and did) make a most excellent witness in divorce court.

It was not until the following June that the case came before Sir Cresswell Cresswell, the first ever President of the Divorce Court, which had only been established six years previous. The proceedings were brief and received only the most perfunctory press coverage. The Rev. Mr. Whipham sought a divorce on the grounds of his wife's "unlawful intimacy" with Philip Rowe. Though Mrs. Whipham was represented by counsel, she chose not to defend her actions. Nor did young Rowe. While having been caught together in bed made the case seem open-and-shut; there were options for the defense. Interestingly, no questions of either condonation on the part of the Rev. Whipham (i.e. he had knowledge of his wife's infidelity and had not acted in a timely manner) or collusion between the Whiphams were raised. In many unhappy marriages, to get a divorce decree, the parties would arrange [collude] for the husband to be caught with "a woman unknown." Certainly, it was socially unthinkable that the Whiphams would collude in the reverse, with *the wife* agreeing to be the compromised party. While a man might recover his place in all but the most censorious quarters of society, the disgrace to the woman would be permanent, also bringing shame upon her children. In the event, Mr. Karslake, the rector's counsel, merely presented a few of the Gidleigh "observers" who swore that Philip Rowe had been "watched into the rectory during the absence of [Mrs. Whipham's] husband." These witnesses provided enough of the required salacious details of the interrupted leg-over to pass the muster required for a divorce. A decree nisi was issued (becoming official in six months) and Sir Cresswell mulcted Philip Rowe, the youthful swain, to pay the bills.

However disgraceful it might be for a clergyman's wife to take a lover in the rectory bedroom (!) or for her clerical husband to lay a trap for her and employ watchers to catch her *en flagrante delicto*, it would not have shocked Sir Cresswell. He was the right man for the job:

> Sir Cresswell had been disappointed and soured in early life in the very matter of marriage, and that gave a cynical turn to his mind, particularly on that very subject.

Since 1857, he had presided over the great rush among unhappily married Britons to seize upon the relaxation of the old divorce laws. This was, for him, just another case. And one of his last, after a fall from his horse, he died in a "fainting fit" a month after the Whipham case was heard.

The jaded judge was one audience; he might be forgiven should he yawn through yet another case. In Gidleigh and Devon, however, the reaction was more profound. This scandalous marriage had now passed beyond unpaid hotel bills and pearl buttons to a squalid case of adultery. This could only reflect back upon the rector. As had been written in *Holiness in the Priest's Household is Essential to Holiness in the Parish*, one of the many clerical guidebooks of the period:

> The Clergyman and his house is as it were a light placed in the parish, to which all eyes are turned for example and guidance. With what passes in an ordinary household the parishioners have nothing to do; but it is natural that they should be anxious to know what passes in their Clergyman's ... If ... *from their own*

observation, they see that such an, "example and pattern of holy living" as he exhorts them to, is not to be seen, even in his own household, then assuredly to him will they apply the apostolic text, "If a man know not how to rule his own house, how shall he take care of the Church of GOD?" and then vain and ineffectual will be his preaching and his exhortations; almost vain will be his labours.

The Rev. Whipham surrendered the living in Gidleigh after the divorce scandal; as "lord of the manor," however, he was allowed to present the church to a clergyman of his choice. In 1865, Whipham was made rector of Hittisleigh, a small village a few miles the other side of Chagford. He died of cancer in November 1882, still living in that "unsuitable cottage" on Holy Street in Chagford. Gidleigh Park was let to a succession of tenants. Whipham's eldest son finally sold the estate in 1918.

As for the Gidleigh lovers, their romance did not survive the scandal. Philip Rowe was apparently banished from the village. He appears in the later census reports working as a "carter" in distant York. Mrs. Whipham did not remarry; she moved to various addresses in London, never far from the home of her married children. She died in 1901. She had been living in Brixton with Laura, who had never married.

His Conduct Has Been Infamous Throughout

Rev A.B. Winnifrith, Curate of Dalwood

THE BLACKDOWN HILLS of East Devon – although justly proclaimed "an area of outstanding natural beauty" – are rarely on the "to-do" lists of those who race on past to the South West each season. The locals, it would not surprise you, are quite willing to live with that. In the absence of the caravans and coaches, the narrow roads through the hills and hedgerows are un-crowded; the isolated villages are unspoiled. However, it is not as if history has passed the area by completely. For, in the last years of the Victorian century, one village in the Blackdown Hills was the scene of a great "clerical scandal."

At the center of a web of country lanes, sits the quiet village of Dalwood, not that many miles northwest of the town of Axminster. St. Peter's is the parish church, one the guidebooks all delight in calling an "ancient edifice" – though a lively debate persists as to whether, in fact, the local pub might be a wee bit older. The Dalwood Fair has been held since first licensed by Edward III in 1345. The vicar of this rustic parish in the 1890's was the Rev. Alfred Vyvyan Cox. However, Dalwood parish was then ecclesiastically linked with Stockland, a village a few miles to the north, even farther into the hills. It was there that the Rev. Cox chose to reside, leaving the Dalwood duties in the hands of his young curate, the Rev. Alfred Baker Winnifrith.

In his late-20's and single, the Rev. Winnifrith was the son of the long-time vicar of Mariansleigh, a village some distance away in North Devon. In Dalwood, the curate was well-liked and quite active. Beyond his liturgical duties, he joined the 3rd Volunteer Battalion of the Devonshire Regiment. He served on the village school board. He was a leader in organizing the various gaieties of rustic village life. Through these latter pursuits, he met the Herns. William Henry Hern was a local miller, Volunteer, and school board member and his wife, Rosa Agnes, was very active in church society. The Herns lived at Dalwood Mill on Corry Brook. Then and now, the Corry flows south providing "an attractive green corridor through the heart of the village greatly enhancing the settlement's rural character." [E. Devon Council, 2007]. Dalwood Mill was owned by Rosa Agnes' father, Hermon Bromfield, a churchwarden at St. Peter's. In a village with fewer than four hundred residents, living mainly on scattered farms, it can be seen that Dalwood church was the center of community life.

That center was fractured in late October 1894 when Rosa Agnes Hern disappeared along with her four-year old son, Stanley. She had ostensibly gone on holiday, taking Stanley to see Mr. Hern's parents. She never arrived. Instead, a "Dear William" letter came by mail to Dalwood Mill – with no trace of a postmark – announcing that she had left him for good and would never give up her son. The Herns had been married since 1889 and it was known by many in the village that their marriage had not been a completely happy one. There would always be theories. At the Dalwood pub, *The Tucker's Arms*, some of the locals over their pints would even give voice to their thought that the curate and Mrs. Hern had been altogether too much in each other's company. Undoubtedly, Hern had heard the same gossip and sought out Mr. Winnifrith and asked of the curate what he knew of his wife's decision to leave him and where she might have gone. Winnifrith admitted that Rosa had explained her intentions to him in a parting letter which he promptly surrendered to William:

> To come straight to the point, I am about to leave Will and am going away by myself to earn my own living. It will be a shock to you I know, and no doubt will grieve you, but I don't think you will be altogether surprised. Will and I have not got on as well as we ought to have done, in fact, I don't think we are at all well-matched, and we have made a mistake. I believe Will has often thought so too.

She also knew that this could make life more difficult for her clerical friend:

> I hope what I am going to do will bring no trouble upon you. It ought not to do so and I should have no fear of it if it were not for the unfounded and annoying tales there have been. If people only knew how often you have tried to smooth things between Will and me, they would not have much to say.

Beyond sharing this letter, Mr. Winnifrith insisted to Hern that he had had no advance word of Rosa Agnes's plans to leave Dalwood and had no idea where she had gone. He also assured the miller that he was sorry to hear of his domestic unhappiness and if he did receive any news about Mrs. Hern, he would forward it to him immediately. Hern recalled that the curate had even offered to serve as a mediator if requested.

Rewards were offered, detectives employed, newspaper advertisements were placed, all to no avail. More than a year passed without word. The Rev. Mr. Winnifrith remained at his duties at St. Peter's. When asked, as he regularly was, he reported having had no contact at all from Mrs. Hern. In November 1895, Winnifirth resigned his curacy and left Dalwood to assist his brother who ran a small school in Kent.

In Dalwood, the locals continued to share their theories and the latest gossip. It was heard said that Will Hern had already fixed his eye on a new young lady but first, of course, he would need to sever ties with the old.

In May 1896, before Mr. Justice Gorell Barnes in London, William Hern sued Rosa Agnes Hern for divorce on grounds of her adultery with the co-respondent, the Rev. Alfred B. Winnifrith, curate of Dalwood.

Mr. Winnifrith understandably felt he had been placed in a very unfair position, left alone to answer this charge. Mrs. Hern was not present to defend herself or him. Still, it was probably not the wisest course of action for Mr. Winnifrith to attend the first day of the divorce proceedings without any legal counsel. William Hern – who was represented by J.C. Priestly - testified that he and Mr. Winnifrith had been intimate friends for some time and he was, at first, reluctant to believe the village rumours. Even his father-in-law had claimed to see the curate and Mrs. Hern embracing. Finally, Hern saw it with his own eyes; he walked in upon his wife, her arms around the curate, while the clerical gentleman's head was resting upon her bosom. Rosa explained that Mr. Winnifrith was suffering from a painful earache and had no one to care for him, "Poor fellow." While Hern admitted that he accepted that tale of consolation, he ordered his wife not to see Mr. Winnifrith alone anymore. He also forced her to return gifts that she had received from the curate. He objected to her private correspondence with the clergyman. After Rosa had left Dalwood, Hern recalled several conversations with Winnifrith who repeatedly denied being guilty of any improper conduct with Mrs. Hern. The curate did confess that Rosa had mentioned to him that she had given thought to leaving her husband, but Winnifrith admitted he had neither made any effort to stop her nor did he say anything to Mr. Hern about those plans until she had gotten away. In fact, in a letter to the miller, Winnifrith bluntly stated, "Pardon me saying it, but my personal observation leads me to the conclusion that you were utterly unsuited to each other." Priestly said he could only call such a letter "the most impudent concoction ever written." The miller said he could not prove that Mr. Winnifrith had been part of the planning for his wife's disappearance but he believed he had "induced" her to leave Dalwood. Hern added that, from what he had learned from others, including most notably the curate's housekeeper, he was now certain that the curate had been guilty of adultery with his wife.

Priestley, having concluded his questioning, turned the witness over for cross-examination. To be sure, courtroom interest was heightened when the Rev. Mr. Winnifrith stood to question his accuser. The curate would attempt to show that the miller's wife had left him for reasons unconnected with her friendship for her clergyman. Hern denied that his was an unhappy marriage. He denied ever claiming Rosa was "unfitted to be a farmer's wife." He denied forcing her to lift a heavy boiler until her blood vessels burst. He admitted that at no time had he ever forbidden his wife to visit or speak to her curate. Hern also conceded that he had never spoken to Winnifrith about any intimacy with his wife until well after she had fled Dalwood.

Hern's testimony took all of the first day. On day two, Mr. Winnifrith was no longer alone, having made the wise decision to hire counsel. Though Mr. Justice Barnes thought the curate had very ably questioned the previous witness, he welcomed to the defense table James Rentoul QC, also the son of a clergyman – albeit an Irish Presbyterian. The next witness for the petitioner (i.e. William Hern) was Mrs. Mary Mears, the curate's housekeeper during his three years in Dalwood. She testified to letters passing back and forth between the vicarage and Dalwood Mill. She was entrusted with delivering some of them. On one occasion, she couldn't help taking a peek inside and saw that the letter began "My darling one." She returned to tell Mr. Winnifrith – by way of a laugh – that she had given the letter to William Hern. She said the curate exclaimed, "My God, my God, I am a ruined man!" Though she quickly assured him it was a joke, she said Mr. Winnifrith was "quite shaky" for several hours. She also recalled that Mrs. Hern was frequently alone with the curate at his lodgings and she often saw them sitting closely together. On one occasion, she walked in and found them on the hearthrug. When she remonstrated with Mr. Winnifrith, he told her that she must understand that Mrs. Hern was a very unhappy woman and he, unlike her husband, truly loved her. She was too beautiful to work in a mill. Well, Mrs. Mears would hear none of that. She told the court that she came right out and told Mr. Winnifrith that if she were Will Hern, she'd throw the curate into the millstream and then go horsewhip his wife.

Rentoul went to work on Mrs. Mears. The housekeeper was living apart from her husband. The name of the father on her child's birth certificate was not that of Mr. Mears. She explained it was a registrar's error. As for the conduct of Mr. Winnifrith, she admitted that Will Hern was also often "alone" with the curate. As village friends, the Herns and Mr. Winnifrith were frequently in each other's company. While she didn't think it proper for Mr. Winnifrith to be so often alone with another man's wife, she conceded that she had never witnessed anything indecent in the curate's conduct toward the lady. Nor did she ever believe that he had committed adultery with Mrs. Hern. Mrs. Mears admitted that she would have given notice if she believed the curate had committed adultery. Yet, she had continued to be his housekeeper until he left Dalwood. She had continued to attend St. Peter's and take the sacrament from the hands of Mr. Winnifrith. Rentoul pressed on further, seeking details of the specifics of the curate's sitting room. Did the door have a lock, was it locked, would she knock, did she knock, how big were the armchairs, where was the hearthrug; questions that continued to the point that Mrs. Mears became ill and had to be excused from the witness box.

The next witness was Hermon Bromfield, Rosa Agnes' father. He testified that he had stopped by Dalwood Mill one evening and through a window he'd seen his daughter in the curate's arms and they were kissing. He testified that he told no one but his wife. Mr. Justice Barnes found that hard to believe, "Why did you not interfere straight off? She was your own daughter. It is most extraordinary." Bromfield said he thought his wife could handle the matter best. Despite this alleged scene, he had continued to serve with Mr. Winnifrith on the school board and as a churchwarden in Dalwood. He had never mentioned this kissing incident until after his daughter had left the village.

The case for Wiliam Hern having concluded, Rentoul opened the defense by saying that the Rev. Alfred Baker Winnifrith had been the victim of groundless village gossip. He had had no advance word of Mrs. Hern's plans to leave her husband and had no knowledge of her current whereabouts. The curate was eager to testify and to absolutely deny every claim that had been made against his moral character. From the witness box, Mr. Winnifrith explained to the court his relationship with the Herns. He had worked closely with the petitioner – Mr. Hern – on the Dalwood school board and Mrs. Hern had frequently assisted him in the planning and execution of various village "entertainments."

A: She was musical.
Q: And you were musical?
A: I am generally considered so.

He added that Mrs. Hern's role in all of these activities had been with the knowledge and approval of her husband. He had never kissed her. He had never sat on a hearthrug with her. He had never helped her off or on with her boots. He had had a nettling earache in 1894 but had sought a doctor not a woman's bosom for comfort. He never told Mrs. Mears that he loved Mrs. Hern. When asked why Mrs. Mears would then have made these charges against her employer, he laughed and said it was his belief that Mrs. Mears was very much interested in seeing Will Hern get his divorce as she had an unmarried daughter who had a fancy for the local miller. He concluded by reiterating that he never had any role in Mrs. Hern's disappearance:

Q: Do you know where she is now?
A: I do not.
Q: Did you know at any time since she left Dalwood where [Mrs. Hern] was?
A: I did not.

Winnifrith was questioned next by Mr. Priestley, the counsel for Hern. The curate denied that he and Rosa had a special friendship. He described her as "passably good looking" and admitted he cared for her but not with any considerable affection. In fact, he insisted that his relationship with Rosa was not unlike those he enjoyed with other women in his parish. That reply produced some ribald laughter in court. Winnifrith conceded that he had formed the opinion that the Herns were unsuited for each other. He had also taken a decided dislike to Rosa's father, Hermon Bromfield. He acknowledged writing a letter to Hern complaining that Bromfield's gossip about the "kissing scene" had "scratched a small scab into a festering sore. Even if I had it in my power, I should have no inclination to help him find his daughter." As for Mrs. Mears, the Rev. Winnifrith cheerfully acknowledged that his housekeeper was a village tale-bearer, yet he had not given her the sack. He said it was a "Hobson's choice," if he had sent her away, she would have simply taken her silly gossip away with her.

Next, for the defense, a letter from the Bishop of Exeter was introduced. His Excellency, the Rev. Edward Bickersteth, allowed as how Mr. Winnifrith's conduct might have been considered indiscreet, however, a panel of local clergy had concluded that there was no reason for any church inquiry into his behaviour. Mr. Winnifrith's clergyman-father testified to having visited Dalwood and having observed that the "greatest possible friendship" had existed between his son and *both* Mr. and Mrs. Hern. The curate's mother testified that Hern had pressed her to urge her son to reveal Rosa's whereabouts. She had told him that if her son had promised to keep Rosa's secret, the rack would not let him break his word. The old clergyman's wife thought that Mrs. Hern had innocently made a confidant of her clergyman as "many women are known to do." She admitted however, "We didn't like the business at all." Winnifrith's brother, who had spent some time staying in the Dalwood vicarage, testified that Mrs. Mears was well-known in the village as a "tattler."

The trial having taken most of three days, the jury was instructed by Justice Barnes who gave every indication of leaning towards the side of the accused clergyman. He cautioned the jurors as to the housekeeper's testimony. Why would he have confided his love for this woman only to the village tattler? He also returned to Bromfield's testimony; would any father have said nothing to his married daughter after seeing her kissing a man not her husband? Still, Barnes said the decision was the jury's: "The future of three people lies in your hands; you must not shrink from your duty, however unpleasant it might be." The jury spent ninety minutes before finding that the Rev. Alfred Baker Winnifirth had committed adultery with Rosa Agnes Hern. William Hern was granted his requested divorce and custody of his son – who along with the child's mother – remained among the missing.

Formally adjudged now as an adulterer, Mr. Winnifrith's clerical career – under the terms of the recently passed Clergy Discipline Act - was over. Hoping at the last to rescue his career and reputation, Winnifrith promptly filed a request for a new trial and – the excitement can well be imagined – he made the sensational announcement that he would be joined in that appeal by Mrs. Rosa Agnes Hern who had just then been located, working as a barmaid at a hotel in Barnsley near Leeds. She had apparently seen a desperation personal ad – taken out only days after the divorce trial - seeking information on her whereabouts. She had immediately been in communication with Mr. Winnifrith's solicitor and was ready now to testify.

Mr. Winnifrith demanded a new trial, citing three grounds. Firstly, the divorce court jury had failed to properly consider the evidence. Secondly, his case had been prejudiced by the absence of the respondent [Mrs. Hern]. Now, in a sworn affidavit, he stated:

> Since the trial, the whereabouts of the respondent as a material and necessary witness for the co-respondent's case has been discovered and I am anxious that her evidence should be before the court.

Finally, he asserted that Mrs. Hern had not even known of the divorce proceedings until she saw the published accounts that followed the trial. In her affidavit, she swore that until she saw a brief mention in *The Sheffield Daily Telegraph*, she had no idea her husband had taken such a course. Then, days later, on 11 May 1896, she saw an item in the personals column of *The Yorkshire Post* and responded to it. She swore that she had then immediately decided to come forward to clear Mr. Winnifrith from the charge of adultery. She insisted that she and the curate had never committed adultery or behaved improperly. She swore that their relationship had gone no further than her shared confidences with him about her unhappiness with her husband. She feared that in any divorce action, she would have lost her son. Her only option had been to leave Dalwood with the boy and start a new life.

> I left my husband on 29 Oct 1894 because of his bad temper and unkindness. The Rev. Alfred Baker Winnifrith was not the cause of my leaving my husband. He did not know of my intention to leave my husband. Nor did he know where I went, or with whom I was living. I have never seen or communicated with him, nor has he communicated with me, or, as far as I know, seen me since I left.

A three-judge Court of Appeal considered the case and Mr. Justice Lindley delivered their ruling on 8 July 1896. Taking the issues raised in reverse order, Lindley thought that Mr. Hern and his solicitors had made every bona fide effort to locate and notify his wife of his intention to sue her for divorce. It was obviously Mrs. Hern's wish not to be found and if an injustice had been done to her, she had brought it upon herself. Without making any direct charges, Lindley was also sceptical of the timing of Mrs. Hern's re-appearance. As for whether her testimony would have changed a thing at the Divorce Court, Lindley stated that he had not been convinced that it would have made any difference. Concluding, he thought the jury had before it "ample evidence" upon which to base its verdict against Mr. Winnifrith. Therefore, the appeal was denied. As for Mr. Winnifrith, Justice Lindley tossed off the parting comment that "it is very plain that he has much to learn before he is fitted for the cure of souls."

For Mrs. Hern, the decision to come forward had an even greater personal impact. She was now ordered to surrender custody of six-year old Stanley to his father. The child was handed over to his father's representatives at St. Pancras Station on 28 July 1896. Furthermore, inquiries were now afoot in Yorkshire. Where had she been exactly since leaving Dalwood some eighteen months earlier? The investigation was soon in the hands of Detective Inspector John Conquest of Scotland Yard. In early December 1896, Conquest had gathered enough information to arrest Rosa Agnes Hern in Leeds and the Rev. Alfred Baker Winnifrith in Hythe, Kent, where he had been teaching at a "boarding school for young gentlemen" run by his brother. On 7 December, Alfred and Rosa stood together in the dock of Bow Street Police Court charged with perjury and conspiracy.

Working backwards from Barnsley, Conquest had been able to trace Mrs. Hern's many movements from the day she left Dalwood Mill for the last time. What was revealed was the very plain truth (at last) that the Rev. Mr. Winnifrith and Mrs. Hern had been together in planning her escape from Devon from the beginning. Having told her husband initially that she was going to see his parents, she went instead to a temperance hotel on the High Street in Ashford, Kent, operated by a Mr. Holton. The innkeeper testified that he knew Mrs. Hern only as a "Mrs. Vernon," a widow who, with her son Stanley, took a bedroom and sitting room in his establishment between October 1894 and August of 1895. Over that period, she was visited several times by a gentleman who was, on some, but not all occasions, dressed in clerical attire. Holton identified both parties in court. He also testified that the gentleman would occasionally spend the night, usually occupying a room directly across the hall. A housemaid at the hotel and a nurse who would occasionally baby-sit the child also swore that they had seen Mrs. Vernon and the clerical gentleman walking together in Ashford.

While in Ashford, Mrs. Hern/Vernon had no visible means of employment. Her bills had been paid by the visiting gentleman who, she had explained, was trustee for some property left to her little boy. However, by August of 1895, perhaps having exhausted Mr. Winnifrith's ability to fund a second household, she sought employment and answered an ad from a Dr. Hughes seeking a housekeeper in Liverpool. She took lodgings with a Mrs. Harper in the Egremont section of that city. Mrs. Harper testified that her new boarder had displayed a photograph in her room of a clergyman, a man the witness could now identify as the former curate of Dalwood. When she asked Mrs. Vernon – for that was the name she continued to use – what had happened to her husband, the "widow" responded that he had been killed by a cricket ball. In the police court, both women smiled briefly at this display of macabre inventiveness.

The situation with Dr. Hughes lasted only a few weeks. Next, Mrs. Vernon managed to find employment as a "ladies companion" for a Mrs. Agnes Cassells in Liverpool. Mrs. Cassells also noticed the photograph of the clergyman and inquired if he was her beau and was told no, he was simply "a curate friend" who had been very nice to her son. Mrs. Cassells had no facilities for a child in her house and so Stanley had remained behind at Mrs. Harper's boarding house. This situation was obviously not a happy one for Rosa. On one occasion, finding her companion crying, Mrs. Cassells asked why and "Mrs. Vernon" admitted that she was not a widow but had run away from her husband. She had just received word that he was going to sue her for divorce, naming the man in the photograph. She was dreadfully afraid of losing her child and was quite worried that she might be traced to Liverpool. Mrs. Cassells – to be sure, eagerly – suggested that Mrs. Vernon had better look for other more remote employment.

The next stop was *The Lord Nelson Hotel* on Shambles Street in Barnsley, Yorkshire, where, in November 1895, a little over a year after leaving Dalwood, Rosa Agnes Hern, a miller's daughter from Devon, was engaged as a pianist-cum-barmaid for ten shillings a week plus board and lodging. Stanley had still remained with Mrs. Harper, being boarded for 6s. 6d. per week. Mrs. Hyde, the landlady at the *Lord Nelson*, testified that she also knew her employee as the widowed Mrs. Vernon. The well-traveled photograph of the gentleman in clerical dress was on display once again. Mrs. Hyde testified that Mrs. Vernon received regular letters, some including postal orders. She was quite sure that Mrs. Vernon burned the letters after reading them. Although the landlady did find one letter carelessly left about in the billiard room. She admitted that a solicitor had since paid her a sovereign for that letter, which was now produced in Police Court. The missive was in Mr. Winnifrith's handwriting and addressed to M.D.R. which was suggested to mean "My Dear Rosa."

You have been getting on all right, I hope, and have not been uneasy at my silence. You must not be. I cannot help but be erratic and brief. You must not write to me until you hear from me, but you may of course, if you have anything of supreme importance to communicate to me, send a blank stamped envelope to Mrs. J., and request her to address it to me at M. You will not adopt this plan unless compelled.

In addition, Mrs. Hyde testified that she had observed that "Mrs. Vernon," for several days in succession, had made clippings from the newspapers. It was proven that the articles clipped pertained to the divorce proceedings involving her husband and Mr. Winnifrith. Mrs. Hyde told the court that some short while later, her pianist/barmaid gave notice, admitting to her that she was indeed the "Mrs. Hern" whose story had been in all the papers. She had decided to go to London to help the man in the photograph.

All of this could only implicate the Rev. Winnifrith. He had clearly been identified as the "gentleman" who had visited "Mrs. Vernon" in Ashford. His handwriting was identified on the letters to "Mrs. Vernon" that had been obtained (and/or purchased.) It was now evident to all that he had been in regular communication with Mrs. Hern. Yet, whenever he had been asked by her husband's solicitors if he had any idea where she might be, he had replied in the negative. In November 1895, he went so far as to send an angry letter to Mr. Hern's representative. He had written that "words were utterly inadequate" to describe his response to such "unwarrantable assumptions." For all he knew she and the child were dead, having left him to face a "vile conspiracy." He added that if Mr. Hern wished to bring him into court, he would welcome the opportunity to expose for the public the campaign of "dastardly persecution" of which he had been the victim.

The final witness in police court was William Henry Hern. He testified of his repeated inquiries of Mr. Winnifrith for any information he may have received from his wife. The clergyman had insisted he was as much in the dark as anyone and professed to share Hern's concern. The husband stated that his wife had no more than £5 to her name when she left him, not enough certainly to have supported herself and her child for the several months prior to finding her first employment in Liverpool.

Cross-examined by Mr. Rentoul, who again appeared for Mr. Winnifrith, Hern denied that he had ever been cruel to his wife. In fact, he considered their marriage to have been a happy one. Rosa Agnes had not

– he testified – threatened to leave him on several occasions. She had not accused him of paying his attentions to other women. Hern also denied the current Dalwood rumour that he was engaged to be married.

The police court magistrate remanded the case for trial; Mrs. Hern was permitted bail but a bid by Mr. Winnifrith's father to bail his son out for the Christmas holiday was rejected. In January 1897, for the third time in less than a year, Mr. Winnifrith was back in court. But now the headlines read: *A CLERGYMAN AND A BARMAID TRIED FOR PERJURY*. Alfred Winnifrith and Rosa Hern were tried in the Old Bailey before Justice Henry "Hanging" Hawkins. They were each charged with perjury and conspiracy to defeat the due course of justice. Mr. Rentoul again appeared for the defendants and entered guilty pleas for both. The prosecutor was Charles Mathews QC.

The prosecutor opened by making the interesting remark that some forms of perjury in the Divorce Court "might not be altogether condemned." The reader is directed to an essay entitled *Common Fallacies of the Sound Mind*, published the same year Alfred and Rosa stood accused in the dock. Henry Maudsley wrote:

> Perjury notoriously counts for nothing, is taken quietly as natural, in the English Divorce Court. A man in good social position, who did not go into the witness box to commit perjury in order to save the reputation of a lady with whom he had committed adultery, might incur severe social condemnation. A code of honour exacts that one of the Ten Commandments be thrown overboard to conceal the breach of another.

Apparently this immunity from prosecution is available only to those "in good social position" and did not extend to a country curate and a miller's daughter. Mathews, of course, pointed out that Mr. Winnifrith held the unique position of a clergyman who had repeatedly lied when asked if he knew the whereabouts of Mrs. Hern. In this case, as the prosecutor suggested to Justice Hawkins, there were no redeeming circumstances.

Mr. Rentoul advised the judge that Mr. Winnifrith stood ready to accept the court's judgment however severe; his only wish was that Mrs. Hern might be spared. She had come forward to swear out a false affidavit only to save him. In the course of that action, she had lost her son. She had suffered enough. As for Mr. Winnifrith, he had also suffered, having been irrevocably turned out of his profession. Counsel closed by begging Justice Hawkins for leniency.

Taking two days to consider his sentence, Justice Hawkins summoned the parties on Saturday, 16 January. He considered the case to be one of grave importance:

> Those who administer the law rely upon the testimony of witnesses given on oath, and if it was not that the law punished perjury with severity, no person's life, property, or anything that he held dear to him would be safe.

As for Mr. Winnifrith, Hawkins said that he had behaved infamously throughout. He had brought disgrace and discredit upon his parents, especially his aged father – a clergyman in the same county. Hawkins said he could find no circumstances of mitigation in Winnifrith's case on account of the atrocity of the offence – his hypocritical falsehoods, he being a clergyman. Limited in the punishment he could impose, Hawkins ordered that Alfred Baker Winnifrith be sentenced to eighteen months hard labour and he harrumphed that he only wished it could have been longer. He had some little sympathy for Mrs. Hern believing she had acted under the influence of the curate. However, what she had done to her husband by removing a child to whom he was "devotedly attached" was very cruel indeed. Therefore, he ordered her to serve six months at hard labour. She was sent to Wormwood Scrubs; it was later reported that her labour there included macramé and beading, "at which industries, she has become quite expert."

Within a fortnight of his ex-wife being sent off to jail, William Hern married again – as had been his plan according to village gossip, of course. He, too, had perjured himself in a way, perhaps forgivably. In February 1897, he married Sarah Seward, a publican's daughter from Stockland. Hern remained a miller in Dalwood.

We can also report that, in late 1899, without any public notice being taken, the co-conspirators and ex-convicts Alfred Baker Winnifrith and Rosa Agnes Hern were married in Croydon. After his release from prison, the erstwhile clergyman had returned to teaching and by 1905 was the headmaster at the Clapham School in South London, remaining there through the First World War.